GREAT CAPTAINS UNVEILED

Captain B. H. Liddell Hart

New Introduction by Russell F. Weigley

DA CAPO PRESS • NEW YORK

Library of Congress Cataloging in Publication Data

Liddell Hart, Basil Henry, Sir, 1895–1970.
  Great captains unveiled / B. H. Liddell Hart: new introduction
by Russell F. Weigley.—1st Da Capo Press ed.
    p.   cm.
  "Unabridged republication of the edition first published in London
in 1927"—CIP t.p. verso.
  ISBN 0-306-80686-X
  1. Military biography. 2. Genghis Khan, 1162–1227—Military leadership. 3. Sabutai, ca. 1172–1245—Military leadership. 4. Saxe,
Maurice, comte de, 1696–1750—Military leadership. 5. Gustaf II
Adolf, King of Sweden, 1594–1632—Military leadership. 6. Wallenstein, Albrecht Wenzel Eusebius von, Herzog von Friedland, 1583–
1634—Military leadership. 7. Wolfe, James, 1727–1759—Military leadership. I. Title.
U51.L53 1996   95-43939
355'.0092'2—dc20   CIP

First Da Capo Press edition 1996

This Da Capo Press paperback edition of *Great Captains Unveiled*
is an unabridged republication of the edition first published in
London in 1927, with the addition of a new introduction by
Russell F. Weigley.

Published by Da Capo Press, Inc.
A Subsidiary of Plenum Publishing Corporation
233 Spring Street, New York, N.Y. 10013

TO

MY WIFE

CONTENTS

vii

INTRODUCTION

No other critic and philosopher of military strategy has approached Basil Henry Liddell Hart in
the skill with which, writing about the sword, he
wielded the pen. No other strategic and tactical
critic is likely to be read for the sheer pleasure
of the reading. Liddell Hart's literary style and
the gratification it offers would alone justify this
reissue of his classic study of six great captains
of the medieval and early modern eras. The
relevance he found in these great captains for
military thought between the World Wars—and
the relevance still to be found near the close of
the twentieth century—is almost a bonus. Those
who know his work are apt to pick up a book by
Liddell Hart simply for the joy of savoring it;
the serious reflections on strategy and tactics
can come later.

While *Great Captains Unveiled* is on the face
of it a study in historical biography, it is appropriate to regard its author first as a military
critic rather than a historian or biographer. Liddell Hart's historical writing is generally accurate enough in its marshaling of the facts of the
past, but the historian ought to be primarily a
seeker of the truth about the past for its own

sake, and Liddell Hart was not. To him, the past was not an area to be explored for the satisfaction of discovering and mapping it. Instead, he used the past as a mine from which to quarry illustrative lessons to support the strategic and tactical ideas he had already formulated.

He chose selectively the facts of history that he recounted. History to him was a weapon to be used in argument—as indeed was his pleasing literary style. Therefore, his interpretation of the meaning of history, and, specifically in this book, of the significance of the great captains, is not necessarily the interpretation that would likely be offered by a historian looking for as close an approximation of objective truth as a human can attain. Liddell Hart instead bent his interpretations to serve his arguments. We have here not so much a portrait gallery of great captains from Jenghiz Khan (Temuchin) to Major-General James Wolfe as a series of self-portraits of Liddell Hart, decking out his military ideas in the robes worn by certain military figures of the past whose concepts and teachings he found useful to the advancement of his own military arguments.

That is, Liddell Hart was more a polemicist than a military historian and biographer. But a major reason why he was an effective polemicist, one of the most influential military intellectuals of our century, lies in the breadth of the historic eras and personalities from which he drew his arguments. He wrote *Great Captains Unveiled* to foster twentieth-century military reforms, but he was unusual in turning to military history from the thirteenth through the eighteenth centuries for the evidence from which to reason. If asked where in history to find military experiences suitable for the instruction of present-day military leaders, most professional historians— let alone military men themselves—would probably limit their researches to the era of the French Revolution and Napoleon at the earliest, with a preference for focusing on the Second World War and later. All of the great captains of this book antedate the French Revolution. Although Liddell Hart was too intent on finding evidence for his preconceptions and discarding the rest of the past to have been a true historian, historians ought to be grateful to him for his insistence on the value of studying the entire past. He found the whole human experience enlightening.

And ranging over the entire span of history did enlighten Liddell Hart. He was seeking preconceived object lessons, but he explored widely enough that his appreciation for the value of all manner of human beings, as well as for all of history, could not help but be expanded. He expressed judgments in this book that appear racist today, about the superior military capabilities of some peoples over others. But he did not

have to await the Japanese triumphs over Euro-
peans and Americans in 1941 and 1942 to recog-
nize that the belief in the inherent military inferiority of Asians to Westerners, still prevalent in
the West when this book was published in 1927,
had to be dismissed as an altogether unfounded
myth. Not only had the Japanese already defeated the Russians in 1904 and 1905, but the
Mongol conquests of which he wrote, continuing
after Jenghiz Khan's death under his general
Sabutai, rolled deep into central Europe and in-
cluded victories over some of the most formidable of medieval European fighting men.

   To be sure, Liddell Hart's use of history as a
quarry from which to mine principally those incidents that would support his preconceptions
did indeed constrict his views. He perceived, in
the Mongols' success with a well-armed, highly
mobile cavalry army, evidence that a combined-
arms force of infantry, cavalry, and artillery is
not necessary. Rather, he believed that the Mongols pointed to the possibility that in modern
war, a single arm—a force of properly designed
and employed tanks—would be sufficient for victory. While Liddell Hart's ideas were less influential in the British Army between the World
Wars than he would have wished (or sometimes
liked to think), his outspoken support of a single-
arm force did, in part, contribute to consistent
mediocrity in the military's combined-arms tactics and doctrine, perhaps the single most con-

spicuous shortcoming of the British Army in the Second World War.

Still, Liddell Hart was correct in urging his gospel of mobility as essential to any chance for achieving decisiveness in war. All the essays in this book rightly emphasize the immense military value of mobility. A highly mobile cavalry, trained and conditioned for unusual endurance, was the central ingredient in the success of the book's initial pair of great captains, Jenghiz Khan and Sabutai. Recognition and application of its value was critical to the achievement of all the other captains in the gallery as well. Maurice comte de Saxe, *maréchal de France*, commended himself to Liddell Hart because unlike the later Napoleon I—a proponent of armies so large that they stifled mobility, who was in many ways anathema to our author—Saxe insisted on the virtues of forces small enough to retain mobility. (He also favored a reintroduction of armor protection for soldiers, which Liddell Hart took as Saxe's endorsement-in-advance of twentieth-century mechanized armored warfare.)

Two prominent commanders of the Thirty Years War figure among Liddell Hart's great captains. Gustaf II Adolf of Sweden—Gustavus Adolphus—is rightly heralded here as the father of the modern army: in terms of officer education, national recruitment, the first effective incorporation of firearms into a tactical system,

but above all for making his system combine fire
and movement, emphasizing the importance of
tactical mobility and especially restoring it to
warfare by abandoning the clumsy Spanish *ter-
cio* of early firearm warfare in favor of smaller,
much more flexible tactical formations. On the
opposing, imperial side in the Thirty Years War,
Albrecht Wenzel Eusebius von Wallenstein (cor-
rectly Waldstein), duke of Friedland, Sagan, and
Mecklenburg, countered the ascendancy that
Gustavus gave the Swedes in battle by becoming
primarily a commander not of battle but of ma-
neuver. Liddell Hart regards Wallenstein as
above all a master of psychology who, rather
than allow the Swedes to enhance their reputation for invincibility by affording them continuing opportunities for victory in battle, eroded
that reputation by using mobility to avoid fighting and losing battles, while frustrating the
Swedes by diverting them from their proper
strategic goals.

In dealing with James Wolfe, his final great
captain, Liddell Hart comes closest to writing
military history in the historian's sense. No
doubt because Wolfe was British, Liddell Hart
made his deepest forays into the primary source
materials here, and he reviews in careful detail
the steps that carried Wolfe to the pivotal day,
September 13, 1759, when at only 32 years of
age and a major-general only by local rank in
North America, he held the fate of the first

British Empire in his hands—and assured its
global dominance by capturing Québec, though
dying in the process. Yet the treatment of Wolfe
is also somewhat disappointing, for there is relatively little of the usual stimulating, opinionated
military criticism to accompany the biographical
sketch. The portrait of an unconventionally stu-
dious and innovative young officer swimming
against the tide in a conservative British Army
must have held special appeal for Liddell Hart
and is drawn with feeling. Still, although we
learn that Wolfe, too, was devoted to mobility as
a key to success in war, and while we learn also
of his efforts to improve training and discipline
and of his uncommon dedication to the welfare
of his soldiers, none of it strikes Liddell Hart's
usual sparks.

This criticism suggests that we should feel
thankful that Liddell Hart was not just another
military historian. Many of that breed could
have done about as well as he did with Wolfe.
Few could have drawn his other portraits, less
meticulous in their historical detail, but lively
and challenging precisely because persuasion
and polemics are their purposes. There are
many good military historians. There was only
one Basil Henry Liddell Hart, the military critic
who used history as the foundation both for a
beautiful prose style and for provoking military
men of the modern era to ponder the teachings

and accomplishments of the great captains of
the past, the better to emulate them.

> RUSSELL F. WEIGLEY
> Philadelphia, Pennsylvania
> April 1995

*Noted military historian Russell F. Weigley is
Distinguished University Professor at Temple
University and the author of many books, in-
cluding* The Age of Battles *and* The American
Way of War.

GREAT
CAPTAINS
UNVEILED

I.

JENGHIZ KHAN AND SABUTAI

I.

JENGHIZ KHAN AND SABUTAI.

THE purpose of this study is to bring to notice
two military leaders whose claims to inclusion
in the rôle of the Great Captains have been
almost entirely overlooked. It deals with two
amazing, if almost unknown, figures. First,
Jenghiz Khan, the founder of the Mongol Empire,
the greatest land power the world has known,
the bounds of which made the empires of Rome
and Alexander appear almost insignificant in
comparison. Second, his great general, Sabutai,
who, after his death, carried the Mongol menace
into the heart of Europe, and shook the fabric
of mediæval civilisation in the West. The study
may serve to show that the strategical ability of
these two leaders is matched in history only
by that of Napoleon; that the tactical methods
of the Mongol Army hold lessons of importance
for present-day students; and finally, it may
convince us that we do wrong to dismiss lightly
the military potentialities of the Orient.

I.

If we study a physical map of Asia and Europe, we can trace a vast belt of open and level territory, though of varying altitudes, which stretches from the Yellow Sea in the Far East to the Baltic Sea and the Danube in the West. This chain of plains and plateaux is practically unwooded, and only broken by a few well-defined mountain ranges. It is the trough of the world's migrations, the path by which the great racial invasions have come to Europe and to China. Along it have passed the trans-continental routes of commerce from the early caravans to the Siberian Railway. But in even greater volume has it been the channel for armies, for it offers few obstacles to movement, and there uniquely the all-essential principle of mobility has full rein.

In the centre of the continent lies the Mongolian Plateau, barred by lofty and inaccessible Tibet from the fertile plains of India, but with comparatively easy access to the rich fields of China to the East, and of Western Turkestan and Russia to the West. Here, in this bare bleak enclosure, is the birthplace of the Turco-Mongol race, and the conditions of their environment have given the race their special

characteristics. The European peoples have become seafarers by reason of their lengthy coast-
lines and close touch with the sea. The Mongolian peoples are horsemen because constant
and far-reaching land movement was necessary
to obtain pasturage, and a warlike race because
the barrenness of the land and the resulting
migrations have brought them into repeated
conflict with other tribes and peoples. Long
before the days of Jenghiz Khan, this lateral
expansion of the Turco-Mongol race, and their
pressure on the peoples who lay to the West,
had produced barbarian invasions which overran
Europe and overthrew the Roman Empire, cul-
minating in the invasions of the Huns. The
Bulgars, and the Magyars of Hungary, are of
the Turco-Mongol race, as are the Cossacks of
Southern Russia. Yet though long separated,
these off-shoots retain the instincts and characteristics of the race. They settle only in open
level country—the plains of Hungary, the steppes
of Russia—which recalls their ancestral pastures.
Their very tribal names are often a reminder
of the essential unity of the race—" Cossack "
is but a corruption of Kasak, which means
" separated from the tribe," and Kirghiz implies
" errants." They share many of the same
physical and social characteristics. They are
essentially a warlike and not an industrial race ;

they do not take kindly to the arts of peace. "Man is born in the house, and dies on the field" is one of their proverbs, and the ties of family and dwelling-place are as nothing to those of military comradeship.

II.

The father of Jenghiz Khan, Yesukai, had attained the overlordship of a congery of Mongolian tribes. His son, Temuchin, to give him his true name, was born in a tent on the bank of the river Onon in 1162 A.D., and succeeded his father at the age of thirteen. A number of the tribes seized the occasion to break away, and the early years of his reign were occupied with the successful endeavour to re-establish his sway. This done, he gradually extended his rule over the whole of the Mongolian steppes. It was then, in 1206, at the age of forty-four, that he assumed the name and title of Jenghiz Khan, which is given by historians almost as many meanings as spellings, the Chinese "Ching-sze"—i.e., perfect warrior—being the most appropriate at least.

In 1213 he overran the Kin Empire in China by a concentric attack by three armies. With his borders now firmly established as far as the river barrier of the Hoang-Ho, his base was secure for an advance towards the West. Here lay the rich and fertile empire of the Shah of Khwarizm (Karismian Empire), which embraced what is to-day Turkestan, Persia, and Northern India. The latter's intrigues, combined with Jenghiz Khan's desire for expansion, brought about a conflict, the signal for which was the Shah's folly in putting to death the envoys of Jenghiz.

III.

Fuller knowledge has dispelled the excuse of mediæval historians that the Mongol victories were due to an overwhelming superiority of numbers. Quality rather than quantity was the secret of their amazingly rapid sequence of successes. Alone of all the armies of their time had they grasped the essentials of strategy, while their tactical *mechanism* was so perfect that the higher conceptions of tactics were unnecessary.

To a unique degree had they attained the " intellectual discipline " preached by Marshal Foch. The supreme command was in the hands of the Emperor ; but once the plan was decided upon, the subordinate generals executed the actual operations without interference, and with but the rarest communication with the supreme command. The nominal command of the various armies was held by royal princes, but the actual control was exercised by generals of experience, of whom the most famous were Chépé and Sabutai in the Western campaigns, and Mukhuli in China. Merit and not seniority was the key to advancement : thus both Chépé and Sabutai rose to high command before they were twenty-five, over the heads of far senior generals.

The organisation of the army was on a decimal basis. The strongest unit was the touman, a division of 10,000 troops, which could act as an independent force. The army was made up by a temporary grouping of toumans, generally three. Each touman was composed of 10 regiments of 1000 men, and each regiment of 10 squadrons, and that again into 10 troops of 10 men apiece.

In addition there was a touman d'élite, the guard, which usually formed a general reserve in the hands of the commander-in-chief. There were also various formations of auxiliary troops.

For their protective equipment the Mongols had an armour of tanned hide in four pieces, composed of overlapping plates, which were lacquered to prevent humidity. The shield was only used when on sentry duty.

Their weapons comprised a lance, a curved

sabre with sharpened point, suitable either for cutting or thrusting, and two bows—one for firing from horseback, and the other, for greater precision, when on foot. They had three quivers, each with a different calibre of arrows for the various ranges. One class could penetrate armour, and the other was suitable against unprotected troops. In addition, their light artillery consisted of various missile-throwing machines, mangonels, and catapults. These were taken to pieces, and formed a pack-artillery. They could fire rapidly and accurately, could go anywhere, and were adequate for open fighting.

Every trooper carried a complete set of tools, individual camp-kettle, and iron ration, for his own maintenance and subsistence in the field. He had also a water-tight bag in which he carried a change of clothes, and which could be inflated for crossing rivers.

The tactics of the Mongol Army were rigid in conception, without the possibility of wide variation, but flexible in execution. They do not afford much encouragement to lovers of *laissez faire* tactics and the uncontrolled licence of subordinates, to whom the suggestion of a " normal method " is anathema. They were indeed built up on a definite framework of tactical moves, so that they resembled an applied battle drill. The analogy is further heightened by the fact that the different manœuvres were directed by signals, so that the delays and upsets caused by orders and messages were obviated. The result of these battle drill tactics was seen in an amazing perfection and rapidity of execution. The Mongol force was a machine which worked like clockwork, and this very mobility made it irresistible to troops far more strongly armed and numerous.

The battle formation was comprised of five ranks, the squadrons being separated by wide intervals. The troops in the two front ranks wore complete armour, with sword and lance, and their horses also were armoured. The three rear ranks wore no armour, and their weapons were the bow and the javelin. From these latter were thrown out mounted skirmishers or light troops, who harassed the enemy as he advanced. Later, as the two forces drew near each other, the rear ranks advanced through the intervals in the front ranks, and poured a deadly hail of arrows and javelins on the enemy. Then, when when they had disorganised the enemy ranks, they retired into the intervals, and the front ranks charged to deliver the decisive blow. It was a perfect combination of fire and shock tactics, the missile-weapon troops firing and disorganising the enemy ready for the shock troops to complete his overthrow. In addition to these

individual missile-weapons, which were sometimes fired by troops dismounted, the Mongols
developed extensively the heavier ordnance;
they were, indeed, the inventors of " artillery
preparation."

IV.

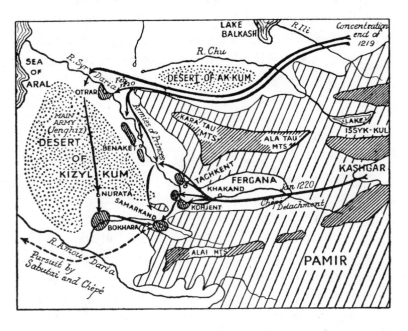

Like all the Mongol campaigns, the invasion
of Turkestan was prepared for by the employment of an extensive spy system, combining
propaganda among the enemy peoples with a
wonderful service of information to the Mongol

command.   The Mongols, indeed, were the pio-
neers in that " attack on the rear " which the
1914-1918 campaign developed.   Meanwhile the
Shah devoted his energies to surrounding Samarkand with immense fortifications, which were
never finished.

Let us now watch the extraordinary skill,
foresight, and grasp of the principles of war
with which Jenghiz Khan gradually unfolded
his plan.   We see him concentrating his main
forces on the Irtish to the east of Lake Balkash.
This was by the Dzungarian Gates, the northern
route into Turkestan.   His first step is security
to his plan.   He covers his concentration, ensures
its secrecy, and avoids the danger of a Persian
offensive by sending his son, Juji, with a force
towards the lower reaches of the Syr Daria
River (the Jaxartes of ancient history).   This
force, in accordance with his instructions, lays
waste the whole trough of country between the
desert of Ak-kum to the north and the Ala-tau
range to the south.   By the time the Shah's son,
the valiant Jelaladdin, arrives on the scene to
meet the supposed invasion, the Mongols have
accomplished their mission, have sent back all
the horses and forage they required, and burnt
the towns and fields.

After a doubtful rearguard battle, the Mongols
set fire to the dry grass on the plain, and dis-

appeared behind the barrier of flame. This was
in the summer of 1219.

For several months there was no further move,
and the Shah prepared his plan of defence. He
mobilised all his vassal states, so that he had
nearly 200,000 men available. But like Napoleon's
opponents he adopted the fatal cordon system.
By stringing out his forces in packets all along
the line of the Syr Daria, he violated the principle
of concentration, and with it those of security
and mobility, for by such a disposition he
restricted himself to a purely defensive rôle.

Then early in 1220, Jenghiz Khan struck his
opening blow, a shrewdly conceived diversion.
Chépé, with two toumans (20,000 men), had
passed by the southern route from Kashgar into
Fergana, and was advancing on Khojent, which
covered the southern end of the Syr Daria line.
Thus Chépé directly threatened the Shah's right
flank, as well as Samarkand and Bokhara,
which lay beyond—the two centres of his power.
It was a dagger pointing at the heart of the
enemy. The Shah reinforced the Syr Daria line,
and concentrated some 40,000 at Bokhara, and
also at Samarkand. Against this Karismian
total of 200,000 the Mongols had about 150,000
in the invading armies. Jenghiz Khan had distributed his main striking force into three armies,
two of three toumans each under his sons Juji

and Jagatai, and the third of three toumans
and the Guard under his direct control, with
Sabutai as his adviser or chief of staff. Chépé's
southern detachment comprised two toumans,
while there were 30,000 auxiliaries distributed
between the four armies.

While Chépé was striking his first blows in
Fergana, the three armies which formed the
main force traversed the devastated route in the
north, and in February suddenly debouched on
the left flank of the Syr Daria line. The speed
of this move was the more remarkable when
we remember that it was made by a mounted
force of more than 100,000, without counting
the pack-animals of the train, and across a country
that had been turned into a desert.

The two armies of Juji and Jagatai turned
south from Otrar, clearing the line of the Syr
Daria, capturing the fortresses, and working
towards Chépé's detachment, which, after taking
Khojent, was seeking to join hands with them.
During the whole of February these operations
on the Syr Daria continued, destroying in detail
the Shah's forces and drawing in his reserves.
Then, like a thunder-clap, as the Shah's attention
was fixed to his front, the horrifying news reached
him that Jenghiz Khan with his reserve manœuvre
had appeared on his left rear, and was almost at
the gates of Bokhara.

This army of 40,000 men, under Jenghiz Khan himself, had followed in the wake of Juji's and Jagatai's armies, crossed the Syr Daria at Otrar, and then—disappeared into the blue. Masked by the armies of the two princes, its arrival on the scene had passed almost unnoticed. Having crossed the Syr Daria, it vanished into the immense desert of Kizyl-kum. By this dramatic venture of 40,000 to 50,000 men, and even more horses, across a supposed impassable desert, Jenghiz Khan gained complete secrecy until the moment when, at the beginning of April, he debouched at the southern end of the desert, took Nuruta, and was almost on the top of Bokhara—in rear of the Shah's armies !

At one blow the Shah's whole line was turned, and his communications severed with his more distant westerly States, whose forces had still to arrive. Demoralised, the Shah fled and left the garrison of Bokhara to its fate. Rarely, if ever, in the history of war has the principle of surprise been so dramatically or completely fulfilled.

On the 11th of April, Jenghiz Khan arrived and captured Bokhara, and then turned east towards Samarkand. Meanwhile, the armies of the princes had joined hands with Chépé, and were converging on Samarkand. The doomed last stronghold of the Karismian power was caught between the hammer of the princes and the anvil of Jenghiz himself, and soon fell.

In the brief space of five months Jenghiz Khan had wiped out an army of 200,000 men, overthrown the mighty Karismian Empire, and opened the gateway to the West, towards Russia and towards Europe.

Every move had been made in calculated and orderly sequence towards the gaining of the ultimate objective, these purposeful moves being finally crowned by the tremendous surprise appearance from the Kizyl-kum Desert in the Shah's rear. A glance at the distances covered reveals the exceptional mobility of the Mongol armies. The sustained and repeated succession of blows was increased by the co-operation between the three columns, each thrust reacting to the advantage of the other columns, so that the economy of force which was manifest in the original distribution was helped by each subsequent link in the chain of events. Thanks partly to the Shah's misguided dispersion of his force, but also to Jenghiz Khan's consummate strategy, the Mongols were able to concentrate in superior force to the enemy at each stepping-stone in their path to final victory. Thus we see Chépé's feint in the south attracting the Karismian attention and their forces, and we admire the

strategic vision which realised that a threat at
this point would most effectively pave the way
for an unhindered debouchement from the Ak-
kum trough.   Again, the advance of Juji and
Jagatai, and their wheel south when they reach
the Syr Daria, skilfully masks the decisive
manœuvre of Jenghiz Khan, and fixes the Shah's
attention to his front along this river line.

Then Chépé, instead of pushing on unsupported towards Samarkand, wheels north to
join the princes, to help in " mopping up " the
Persian " packets " along the river.   When their
rear is thus secure, the combined armies converge
on Samarkand just as Jenghiz Khan advances
on it from the rear, so that the two jaws of the
Mongol Army close with overwhelming superiority
of force on this final enemy position.

In these brilliantly conceived and harmoniously
executed operations we see each of the principles
of war—direction, mobility, security, concentration, and surprise—woven into a Nemesis-like
web in which are trapped the doomed armies of
the Shah.

V.

The enemy armies crushed, Jenghiz Khan despatched Sabutai and Chépé westwards in pursuit of the Shah and to open up the path to further conquests. Jelaladdin still held out in the south for a time, and then crossed the Indus. Jenghiz followed him up, and in 1221 sent an expedition to Delhi, which took nominal possession of the country that his successors were to hold in reality.

Then Jenghiz devoted his remaining years until his death in consolidating his mighty empire, which stretched from Korea to the Persian Gulf. The administration was thoroughly organised, and perhaps the most striking feature of this empire was the complete religious toleration. Among his councillors were to be found Christians, Pagans, Mahommedans, and Buddhists.

Their mission of pursuit accomplished, and the Shah's treasure captured, Sabutai and Chépé asked permission for an advance towards the Kiptchak country—i.e., Southern Russia. The suggestion found instant favour with the Emperor, and in six months they had advanced as far as Tiflis, crushing the kingdom of Georgia. In the spring of 1221 they pressed on into South Russia

as far as the basin of the Donetz.   Everywhere
they established a stable military and civil
administration.   Further, they organised an elaborate system of information to discover the
weak points and rivalries of Europe.   In this
they found the Venetians quite willing to sacrifice
the interests of Christian Europe in order to
gain an advantage over their great trading rivals,
the Genoese.   In return for Mongol help in ousting
the Genoese trade-centres in the Crimea, the
Venetians acted as part of the intelligence service
of the Mongols.

In 1223, however, Sabutai and Chépé were
recalled by Jenghiz Khan, and returned by the
northern end of the Caspian Sea.

The schemes of European conquest were sus-
pended for a generation owing to the death of
Jenghiz Khan in 1227.

Disputes over the succession, for which Jenghiz
had designated his second surviving son Ogdai,
retarded further expansion to the West.   Jenghiz
Khan had called to his aid, in the administration of the immense newly gained empire, Yeliu
Chutsai, a statesman of the former Kin Empire.
The natural result was to give a Chinese complexion to the policy of the Mongol Empire,
and to discourage adventures in Europe.   But
eventually Sabutai's scheme for the invasion of
the West came to the front once more.   The

ground had already been prepared for it by his network of spies and propagandists. The Pope, hopeful of a triumph of mass conversion, a proportion of the Mongol armies being already Nestorian Christians, held aloof from any attempt to proclaim a Holy War. But while Sabutai knew his Europe, and pulled the wires on which danced the royal puppets of Western civilisation, the latter remained in stupid oblivion of the plans and methods of their Mongol invaders. To quote Professor Bury : " The Mongols embarked upon the enterprise with full knowledge of the political situation of Hungary and the condition of Poland—they had taken care to inform themselves by a well-organised system of spies ; on the other hand, the Hungarian and Christian powers, like childish barbarians, knew hardly anything about their enemies," until in a dramatically swift and overwhelming campaign their armies were broken in pieces and their countries overrun. When, owing to events in distant Asia, the Mongols withdrew and the nightmare pall of terror was lifted from Central Europe, there was left just an incoherent sense of a fearful and irresistible tidal wave of yellow hordes. It was then that arose the fictitious excuse of overwhelming numbers, put forward by the mediæval historian to save the reputation of European chivalry. Actually, it is probable that the invading force did not number more than 150,000 men, even when it set out, and that as a result of the losses in the preliminary campaigns and the detachments left to guard the communications with the East, little more than 100,000 took part in the Polish and Hungarian campaigns.

The troops themselves came mainly from China, as the occupiers of the former Karismian Empire were needed for events there. The horses only could be provided from South Russia, which had been organised as a vast remount depôt.

In 1239 Central Russia was subdued as far as Moscow, and security assured to the rear and communications of the invaders. The real objective was Hungary, for its people were the only branch of the Turco-Mongol race who still remained outside the authority of Jenghiz Khan's successors. But the neighbouring powers were likely to resist the invasion, notably Poland, Bohemia, and the Holy Roman Empire, to which Hungary acted as a bulwark. With these powers were arrayed the German military orders, whose mission it was to be the outposts of the West against the heathen.

VI.

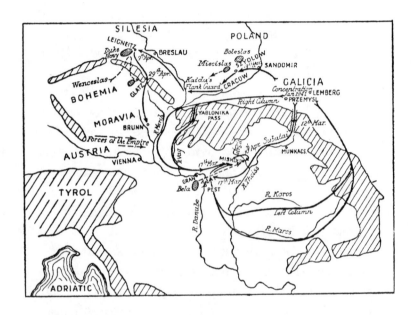

In January 1241 Sabutai concentrated the
Mongol Army in the region Lemberg-Przemysl,
so familiar to students of the World War. His
intention was, like the Russians of 1914-1915,
to force the passes of the Carpathian barrier,
and to march on the Hungarian capital, Gran.
But whilst he thus made his main effort against
the principal enemy, it was necessary to assure
security against interference from the other
powers. An advance into Hungary, with the

Poles and Germans ready to fall on his right flank, would be hazardous. It was necessary to crush these threats to his flank, and to ward off any premature intervention from Austria (the Empire) or Bohemia. The tremendous victories of Szydlow in Poland and Liegnitz in Silesia have caused some historians to imagine that the Mongol purpose was a general conquest of Europe. But Sabutai was far too wise to advance into the hilly and wooded regions of Western Europe, where the Mongolian horsemen would be at a disadvantage, and their system of tactics unsuitable to the country. The plain of Hungary was his goal, and he kept to it unswervingly. It is an object-lesson for modern political strategists who frame their foreign and imperial policies without reference to their military means and limitations.

He divided his force into four armies, each roughly of three toumans. Three of these he assigned to the main operation, and the fourth he used to achieve his secondary or auxiliary objective—the removal of the danger on his right flank. This last, under the Prince Kaidu, moved first, as had Chépé's detachment into Fergana. At the beginning of March 1241 it crossed the Vistula at Sandomir, which it took by storm. Then on the 18th of March it fell upon the Polish armies of Boleslas and Miecislas

at Szydlow and crushed them, driving off the
débris of the two armies in divergent directions.
Kaidu swept on at hurricane speed, took Cracow,
and then Breslau ; on the 8th of April he met
at Liegnitz the German forces under the Duke
Henry of Silesia, together with the orders of
the Templars and Hospitallers, and the remains
of the Polish troops. A day's march to the south
was the army of King Wenceslas of Bohemia.
The Mongols, who were inferior in numbers to
the troops of Duke Henry, struck on the 9th
of April before the allied armies could effect a
junction, and inflicted a terrible disaster. In
less than a month the Mongols had covered some
400 miles, fought two decisive battles, taken
four great cities, and conquered Poland and
Silesia from the Vistula to the borders of
Saxony.

When Wenceslas of Bohemia had news of the
Liegnitz disaster, he fell back to Glatz to cover
his own kingdom. His hope of entrapping the
Mongols in the defiles of Glatz proved vain, for
the latter's reconnaissance warned them of the
trap. Instead, under cover of a mobile screen,
they laid waste Moravia to create, according to
their method, a desert which would guard their
flank. Their purpose accomplished, they turned
south to join Sabutai, ready to fall upon the

flank of the Austrian forces should the Emperor move to the aid of Hungary. But while they had been fulfilling this final phase of their mission of security, Sabutai had wiped out the Hungarian army.

VII.

While Sabutai had taken the foregoing measures to ensure flank security, his grasp of war and its unforeseen happenings had led him not to rely exclusively on it. He advanced into Hungary in three columns, of which the two flank columns traversed the circumference of an elongated circle, while he himself with the central mass started later and went through the diameter. Thus he set up his forces in a close-linked and secure system with true economy of force, as was later the Napoleonic method. The dates of departure and the routes were evidently so arranged that the three columns should converge and join hands on the Danube near the Hungarian capital, where the main enemy forces were likely to be met. The plan was carried out like clockwork. The right column moved westwards to the north of the Carpathians, its exposed flank covered directly by the Vistula and indirectly by Kaidu's flank detachment, then crossed the mountains by the pass of Jablonika and neighbouring passes, and in two bodies turned south-west down the banks of the March and Vag rivers. Sweeping round in a long curving advance, it guarded the right flank of the main army against interference from Austria, until on the 17th of March it joined Sabutai near Gran.

Meanwhile the left column had executed a circular sweep to the south-east through Transylvania until it also rejoined Sabutai, on the 3rd of April.

The central mass—the last to move,—strengthened as usual by the Guard, forced the pass of Ruska on the 12th of March, and advanced by the valley of the Theiss to the Danube near Gran. Rarely, if ever, in history has the speed of its advance been approached. Sabutai's advanced-guard arrived at the Danube on the 15th, and he himself with the main body came up on the 17th of April.

In three days the advanced-guard had covered 180 miles through a hostile country deep in snow! By the 4th of April, Sabutai, his three armies assembled, faced across the Danube Bela of Hungary, who had an army of 100,000 men.

At this moment, however, Kaidu's detachment had yet to fight the battle of Liegnitz, and Sabutai would be uncertain of the situation as regards the other allied armies. Moreover, it would have been difficult for him to force the crossings of the river under the eyes of the enemy, nor would it have been wise to fight a decisive battle with the Danube at his back. Bold as he is in execution—the very embodiment of the principles of mobility and concentration,—his every move is guided by the principle of security. We see him executing a true strategic retreat towards his base at Munkacz, luring on his enemy away from the protection of the Danube and the chance of reinforcement. The retirement is carried out slowly, taking six days to reach the Sajo River, half the distance. Then suddenly he delivers his crushing surprise blow. In the night he crosses the Sajo, and at daybreak on the 10th of April he strikes. By mid-day the Hungarian army has ceased to exist, Bela is in flight, and more than 70,000 of his men are left dead on the battlefield.

Be it noted that it is the morrow of Liegnitz, away in distant Silesia. We are ignorant of the Mongol means of intercommunication, but such synchronisation as is seen here, as also in the junction of the three columns on the Danube, and in the coincidence of Sabutai's own departure with the first successes of Kaidu's detachment in Poland, can hardly be matters of chance.

VIII.

For this battle we have accounts sufficiently reliable to grasp the Mongol tactics. Contemporary observers are impressed, above all, by two features: first, the speed, silence, and mechanical perfection of their evolutions carried out by signals with the black-and-white flags of the squadrons; second, the deadliness of their fire. Their opponents, in the words of a chronicler, " fell to the right and left like the leaves of winter." The armies of the Middle Ages, until the English archers in the next century, relied almost entirely on shock tactics. But the Mongols, as Plano Carpini says, " wounded and killed men and horses, and only when the men and horses are worn down by the arrows, do they come to close quarters." It is the first time in military history that " fire " is employed systematically to pave the way for the assault.

In this battle, while the Prince Batu, the nominal commander, delivers a frontal attack, Sabutai crosses the river lower down, and falls on the flank and rear of the enemy. He had, the day before, reconnoitred and found a ford. Before dawn, Batu seizes the bridge over the river to his front, and covers the passage of his troops by the fire of his catapults and archers.

Then the attack is launched, the enemy are
fixed, when suddenly Sabutai's surprise blow
takes the Hungarians in rear. Magyars, Germans, Croats, and French volunteers all are
cut to pieces; the Knights Templars die fighting to the last man.

IX.

After this holocaust, Hungary was occupied
without further fighting. An organised administration was set up, and the land settled down
under its new conquerors. There was no attempt
to push farther into Europe, apart from one
reconnaissance into Austria, which, strangely
enough, was carried out under an English Knight
Templar who held command in the Mongol
Army.

But at the end of the year Ogdai died at
Karakorum, and the princes were all eager to
compete for the succession. On this account the
Mongol armies and their leaders decided to
return East. The evacuation of Hungary was
carried out systematically and without interference. As a final gesture to show their contempt for the Holy Roman Empire, and to
dispel any idea that they were being forced to

retire, the Mongols sent an expedition to ravage Eastern Austria before leaving.

Nor did this evacuation mean any diminution of their influence, for Ogdai's successor received the homage and embassies of the world. The great commander himself, Sabutai, when he felt old age creeping on, took his leave of the Mongol court, and retired to die alone, in his tent, on the northern steppes. From China to the Danube " he had conquered thirty-two nations and won sixty-five pitched battles."

What is the value of this fragment of history to us, and what are its practical lessons ? In the first place, it dissipates the illusion that Europe alone is the home of military genius. The Japanese have reminded us that courageous and disciplined fighting troops can come from the Orient, but the Mongol campaigns reveal to us that Asia has also produced consummate military leaders who in strategical ability may vie with any in history. What she has done in the past, it is possible for her to do again.

Again, as very perfect exemplars of the principles of war in practice, the Mongol campaigns are of great value in helping students of war to understand what these principles actually mean when translated into definite operations, which is a very different matter from being able merely to recite them like a catechism.

Next, we come to the features of the Mongol tactics and organisation. Their continuous run of victories, usually over superior numbers, were achieved in defiance of most of the canons on which European armies, of the present equally with the past, have based their systems. Nor can these successes be discounted in the way that is common when discussing victories over Asiatic troops, who are regarded as lacking the staying power, discipline, and equipment of European soldiers. Sabutai's warriors proved themselves more than a match for the finest men-at-arms of mediæval Europe, who had superiority both of numbers and armour. The Mongol tactics were to avoid closing with the adversary until he was weakened and disorganised by fire. If charged by the heavy European cavalry, they never let themselves be drawn into a clash, but dispersed on a signal, rallied by signal at a distance, and again assailed the enemy with fire, repeating the process until the phase of " usure " was complete, and the way paved for a decisive charge. Thus they proved that mobility is the king-pin of tactics, as of strategy ; that lightly armed troops can beat more heavily armed ones if their mobility is sufficiently superior, demonstrating that the " weight " of a force is its weapon-power *multiplied* by its mobility, and that this mobility is a

far better protection than armour or any such
form of negative defence.   In naval parlance,
the battle cruiser is superior to the battle-
ship.

Another canon that they tore up was that
mobile troops, such as cavalry, must needs rest
on a stable infantry base.   Although cavalry
was the decisive arm alike of Alexander and
Hannibal, it formed merely the mobile wings
hinged on an essentially protective infantry
centre, which was the pivot on which it man-
œuvred.   The prime feature of the Mongol
military system was therefore its simplicity, due
to the use of a single arm, in contrast to the
inevitably complex organisation of a combination of several arms which has always characterised European armies.   In this way the Mongols
solved the ever-difficult problem of co-operation
between arms which have radically different
qualities and limitations.   The single arm they
used was that which possessed the highest
degree of mobility, and in this lay the secret of
their unbroken run of victory.   At such local
points where greater loco-mobility was needed
than mounted troops could achieve, a proportion of the troops were temporarily dismounted
and fought on foot.

Is there not a lesson here for the armies of
to-day ?   Mobility was the weakest point in the

World War. The armies of Europe were relatively
as immobile as those of the Shah of Karismia and
mediæval Christendom, because they based their
organisation on a multiplicity of arms, and tied
their mobile arms to the service of the less
mobile. The development of mechanical fire-
power has negatived the hitting power of cavalry
against a properly equipped enemy. But on
land the armoured caterpillar car or light tank
appears the natural heir of the Mongol horse-
man, for the " caterpillars " are essentially mechanical cavalry. Reflection suggests that we
might well regain the Mongol mobility and
offensive power by reverting to the simplicity
of a single highly mobile arm, employing the
crews to act on foot as land marines wherever the special loco-mobility of infantry is
needed.

Further, aeroplanes would seem to have the
same qualities in even higher degree, and it
may be that in future they will prove the successors of the Mongol horsemen.

A study of the Mongol methods and the
secrets of their success may at least serve to
clear our minds of long-inherited prejudices, and
reveal the unsoundness of conventional objections to a new and mobile arm which are based
on its minor limitations for movement in certain
localities and over occasional types of ground.

The deduction from the Mongol campaigns would surely seem to be that superior general mobility when allied with hitting power is both a more powerful and a more secure tool than the mere loco-mobility and defensive power of an army founded on infantry.

II.

MARECHAL DE SAXE—MILITARY PROPHET

II.

MARECHAL DE SAXE—MILITARY PROPHET.

In the long roll of the celebrated captains of war, few careers have been so overlooked by military historians as that of Maurice, Count of Saxony, better known perhaps as Marshal Saxe. This omission is the more curious, because Saxe lives not only in his deeds but in his words; for as a military thinker and prophet his outlook was so original, his expression so unfettered by convention, that his writings enjoy a perennial freshness and appeal to the modern spirit of scientific inquiry.

The reasons for the neglect are probably twofold : first, that the wider political interest of Frederick the Great's almost contemporary career focussed on the latter the attention of the general historian ; second, that the historical sections of the Continental General Staffs, blinded by the brilliance of Napoleon, regarded his first campaign of 1796 as the year one of modern

military history, and affected a contempt for all
his predecessors because of the contrast between
their less decisive methods and the " absolute
war " waged by Napoleon.

In a world exhausted—like France in 1815—
through the attempt to copy slavishly the
Napoleonic method, the present may be a fitting
moment to revive the study of a commander in
some respects so akin to that great master, and
in others so strongly contrasting.

In its human interest, few careers and fewer
minds are more arresting than that of this
natural son of Augustus II. of Saxony, for Saxe
was a man built on the large scale—in his physique, in his intellect, in his outlook, and in his
excesses.

A year after his birth, in 1696, his father was
elected King of Poland, but owing to the un-
settled state of the country, Saxe spent his
youth mainly in other lands. At the tender age
of twelve he was present at Malplaquet with the
army of Prince Eugene, and two years later his
impetuous courage was so reckless as to call
upon him the friendly reproof of this famous
leader. In 1711 he received the formal recognition of his father and the rank of count. After
serving under Peter the Great against the Swedes,
and later against the Turks, he went, when
twenty-three, to Paris to study mathematics,

and there took a commission in the French Army. Brilliant service for his new king, interrupted by an adventure in Courland, made him a lieutenant-general when the War of the Austrian Succession opened in 1741. His night surprise and capture of Prague made him famous, and the fact of his exploits being the only redeeming feature of this unsuccessful invasion of Austria led to his being made Marshal of France. After being appointed in 1744 to command the expedition intended to invade England on behalf of the Young Pretender, which, however, was abortive, he turned to the Netherlands, where he won his memorable victory over the British and their allies at Fontenoy. An unbroken series of successes until the end of the war saw Turenne's old title of " Marshal-General of the King's camps and armies " revived for him, but two years later he died at Chambord of " a putrid fever." He left several illegitimate children, among them one whose great-granddaughter was George Sand.

Seven years after, his ' Reveries on the Art of War ' were published posthumously—a military classic that forms the subject of this study. The reader may judge whether Carlyle's extraordinary criticism of it as " a strange military farrago, dictated, as I should think, under opium," has any justification.

That Marshal de Saxe was very different in outlook to that type of traditional soldier who regards his profession as a sacred mystery, beyond the lay comprehension, is well shown by his Preface, in which he declares with regard to war as a science that " custom and prejudice, confirmed by ignorance, are its sole foundation and support. All other sciences are established upon fixed principles . . . while this alone remains destitute."

Nearly two centuries have passed since he wrote this, and yet it is only since the World War that our official Field Service Regulations have, for the first time, attempted to define what are the principles of war—and even then with the sketchiness and dubiousness that denote the ploughing of virgin soil. Writers on war seem to have changed little since Saxe wrote : " So far from meeting with anything fundamental amongst the celebrated captains who have written upon this subject, we find their works not only altogether deficient in that respect, but, at the same time, so intricate and undigested, that it requires very great parts, as well as application, to be able to understand them." . . . " The mechanical part of war is insipid and tedious in description, of which the great captains being sensible, they have studied to be rather agreeable than instructive in their writings upon the subject ; the few books which treat of war as an art, and that furnish us with any principles, are but in small esteem . . . while those which treat of it in the historical way meet with a general good reception."

The student of the military writings of recent generations may recognise the continuity of the two types—on the one hand, the pleasant-to-read but superficial memoirs and commentaries ; and on the other, the massive tomes occupied with a ponderous and minute recital of details, lacking in any synthesis.

No modern critic of authority could hope to surpass Saxe in the pungency and conciseness with which he exposes the traditional way that doctrines have been arrived at : " Blindly adopted maxims, without any examination of the principles on which they were founded . . . our present practice is nothing more than a passive compliance with received customs, to the grounds of which we are absolute strangers."

Since the war of 1914-18 we have been reminded how, twenty years before, Monsieur Bloch, the civilian banker of Warsaw, formed a far truer picture of a war between nations in arms, and foresaw both its nature and its course more accurately, than did any of the General Staffs of Europe.

If, however, instead of following the " blindly

adopted maxims" of military theorists of the
nineteenth century, these General Staffs had
weighed the opinions of Marshal Saxe—one of
that pre-Napoleonic school so despised by them,
—they might at least have avoided some of their
subsequent errors that cost so heavy a price in
lives and money.

As a first example, let us take the cult of
'numbers." On this subject Saxe says: " I
am persuaded that the advantages which large
armies have in point of numbers are more
than lost in the extraordinary encumbrance, the
diversity of operations under the jarring conduct
of different commanders, the deficiency of provisions, and many other inconveniences which
are inseparable from them." " M. de Turenne
was always victorious with armies infinitely
inferior in numbers to those of his enemies,
because he could move with more ease and
expedition." Marshal Saxe understood, like
Napoleon later, that mobility is the predomi-
nant factor in war, and that rapidity of movement, ease of manœuvre, and efficient supply
are the primary conditions to be fulfilled. There
is a striking and thought-provoking parallel
between Napoleon's famous saying that his
victories were won by the legs of his soldiers
and Saxe's dictum half a century earlier, that
" the principal part depends upon the legs and

not the arms: the personal abilities which
are required in the performance of all manœuvres, and likewise in engagements, are totally
confined to them, and whoever is of a different
opinion is a dupe to ignorance, and a novice
in the profession of arms."

Saxe's ideal army—in view of the conditions
of his day—was one of some forty-six thousand
men, and he declares that " a general of parts
and experience commanding such an army will
be able to make head against one of an hundred
thousand, *for multitudes serve only to perplex
and embarrass.*"

Few facts stand out more clearly from the
history of 1914-18 than the powerlessness of
the high commands to attain decisive successes—
a condition due to the unwieldy masses allowing
neither opportunity nor room for manœuvre—
and the constant stultification of offensives owing
to the difficulty of supply. The commanders
of the World War were as unhappily placed as
the proverbial puppy with a tin can attached
to its tail.

The art of generalship as understood by the
great captains was suffocated in infancy by the
weight of the numbers which enwrapped it;
the artist yielded place to the artisan. Watching
it from across the Styx, Marshal Saxe can be
imagined as uttering that quotation from the

Chevalier Folard of which he was so fond:
" War is a trade for the ignorant and a science
for men of genius."

The great captains, however, *created* opportunities for manœuvre; they did not wait,
Micawber-like, in the hope that " something
would turn up." Useless though it is to cry
over the spilt milk of the World War, it is nevertheless the part of wisdom to profit by experience, and in this respect the attitude of our
former enemies is both an example and a warning.
One of the axioms of military history is that
armies learn more from defeat than victory—
the German military power was forged in the
years when the German states lay under the
heel of Napoleon; 1870 gave birth to the renaissance of French military thought which
culminated in Foch; the disasters of the Boer
War produced that highly trained instrument,
the British Expeditionary Force of 1914. Thus
it is but natural that, more than any other,
the present German military doctrine embodies
this supreme lesson of the bitter years of the
World War—that quality, attained through in-
tensive and scientific training and expressed in
a supreme degree of mobility and the fullest
exploitation of manœuvre even by the smallest
units of infantry, will more than compensate
for the greater numbers of a short-service army.

It has been well said that " the Germans went
to Cannæ for their last model ; they will go to
Cunaxa for their next."

Another mistake, paid for heavily in 1914,
of which Marshal Saxe foresaw the dangers
and warned his pupils of the folly, was the
construction of permanent fortifications around
cities. " I look upon the works of nature to be
infinitely stronger than those of art: what
reason therefore can we plausibly assign for
neglecting to make a proper use of them ?
Few cities have been originally founded for the
purpose of sustaining a siege ; but were indebted
to trade for their largeness, and to chance for
their situation . . . There is another more
powerful reason to persuade me that fortified
cities are capable of making but a weak defence,
which is, that notwithstanding a garrison is
furnished with provisions for a three months'
siege, yet it is no sooner invested than they
find that there is hardly a sufficient quantity
for eight days ; because no extraordinary allow-
ance is made, in the calculation of numbers,
for ten, twenty, or perhaps thirty thousand
additional persons, who have abandoned the
country . . . to find refuge there . . . Some
may perhaps observe that those who could
not furnish their own provisions should be
expelled the garrison ; but such an inhuman

proceeding would be attended with more misery
and distress than even the arrival of the enemy.
But suppose nevertheless it be put into execution,
is it probable that when the enemy invests the
place he will suffer these wretches to retire
where they please and the garrison to avail
itself of their banishment ?   So far from it,
that he will undoubtedly turn them back again ;
and surely the governor will not suffer them
to perish with hunger at the gates ; neither can
he be afterwards able to justify such conduct
to his sovereign . . . What I have been saying
appears to me sufficient to demonstrate the great
defects of fortified cities : and that it is most
advantageous to erect fortresses in such situations as are strong by nature, and properly
adapted to cover the country, after having
done which it will become a matter of prudence,
if not to demolish the fortifications of towns,
at least to relinquish all thoughts of strengthening them for the future, or of laying out such
immense sums of money to such useless and
ineffectual purposes.

" Notwithstanding that what I have here
advanced is founded upon sense and reason,
yet I am conscious there is hardly a single
person who will concur with me, so prevailing
and so absolute is custom : a place situated
according to my plan may be defended against

an enemy for several months, or even years, because it is free from that detriment and encumbrance which is unavoidably caused by citizens." To-day military thought is at one with Marshal Saxe in the opinion that natural sites should be selected for permanent defences, and that cities should be left unfortified.

The survivors of a war that witnessed the revival of armour in the form of the steel helmet and the tank—at last partially realising the folly of pitting flesh and blood against machine-guns and of exposing cloth-covered heads to shrapnel bullets and splinters—may be interested in the Marshal's views on the discarding of this protection. " I am at a loss to know why armour has been laid aside, for nothing is either so useful or ornamental. Perhaps it may be said that the invention of gunpowder abolished the use of it, but that is far from being the true reason, because it was the fashion . . . to the year 1667, and every one knows that powder was introduced amongst us long before that time. I shall endeavour to make it appear that its disuse was occasioned by nothing but the inconvenience of it.

" I have invented a suit of armour, consisting of thin iron plates fixed upon a strong buff-skin, the entire weight of which does not exceed thirty pounds . . . and although I cannot allege it to be proof against a ball, especially one that is fired point-blank, nevertheless it will resist such as have not been well rammed down, or are received in an oblique direction. . . . By arming your cavalry in this manner they will rush upon the enemy with irresistible impetuosity, grown doubly desperate from a consciousness of their own security, and a thirst of revenge for the dangers they have just escaped. And how can those whose bodies are quite unguarded be able to defend themselves against others who are, in a manner, invulnerable ? . . .

" This kind of armour will not only have a good effect to the eye, but reduce the expense of the clothing considerably, for nothing more will be required than a small buff-skin every six years, a cloak every three or four, and a pair of breeches. The hat is to be exchanged for the Roman helmet, which is so graceful that nothing can be comparable to it, and it lasts, as does also the armour, during a man's life. Thus the dress will be rendered much less costly and more ornamental ; your cavalry will be fired, from a sense of their superiority, with an eagerness to engage the enemy. . . . I should not be surprised to see ten or a dozen such horsemen attack and defeat a whole squadron, because fear would prevail on one side, and courage on the other."

Then follows a passage which would seem applicable to the argument used by the opponents of tank warfare : " To say then that the enemy will adopt the same measures is to admit the goodness of them ; nevertheless they will probably persist in their errors for some time, and submit to be repeatedly defeated, before they will be reconciled to such a change, so reluctant are all nations to relinquish old customs. Even good institutions make their progress but slowly amongst us, for we are grown so incorrigible in our prejudices that such whose utility is confirmed by the whole world are notwithstanding frequently rejected by us, and then to vindicate our attitude we only say, ' 'Tis contrary to custom.' "

Marshal Saxe then points out that even if when the armour is penetrated a severer wound ensues, which he doubts, the balance is still greatly in its favour, " for what will signify the loss of small numbers thus occasioned by their armour provided that, in general, it gives us the superiority over our enemies and wins our battles ? "   " Nothing but indolence and effeminacy could have occasioned its being laid aside : to carry the cuirass during the whole year for the uncertain service of a single day was deemed perhaps a hardship ; but when a State so far degenerates as to suffer . . . convenience to supply the place of use, one may venture to foretell, without the gift of prophecy, that its ruin is approaching." Saxe's words hold a truth of wide import, not only to military questions, but to the political problems of our own State to-day. He continues: "The Romans conquered the world by the force of their discipline, and in proportion as that declined their power decreased . . . and those very barbarians, whom they had formerly defeated in such numbers, and who had worn their yoke during so many ages, became then their conquerors."

In the military sphere, Saxe's arguments for the revival of armour could hardly be improved on, and to-day, when these two defects are removed in great measure by the fact that armoured protection is now no longer muscle-moved but mechanically moved and bullet-proof in addition, it is tragic to reflect upon the array of military opinion which still contemplates pitting large masses of unprotected flesh and blood against machine-guns.

No maxim is more quoted than Napoleon's dictum that "the moral is to the physical as three to one," yet none surely seems so little understood. There can be little surprise at the decisive results when tanks were present in the later engagements of the World War as compared with those of the earlier years when the infantry depended on artillery support. As a fortifier of moral an immediate and visible form of support is infinitely more efficacious than a distant and unseen one. Few have grasped more clearly than Saxe how delicately is poised the balance between the will to go forward and the instinct to seek safety in flight, and that confidence or its decline is most often the deciding factor in the scales. Nothing strengthens confidence more than the feeling of close support, and this Saxe must have appreciated when he wrote: " I am persuaded that unless troops are properly supported in an action they must be defeated . . . because it is natural for every man, who sees danger before him and no relief behind, to be discouraged; and this is the reason why even the second line has sometimes given ground while the first was engaging, . . . and although it seems hitherto to have escaped the reflection of any, cannot, as I have already observed, be imputed to any other cause than the frailty of the human heart." His solution, in those pre-tank days, was to place small bodies of heavy-armed cavalry close *in rear* of the infantry, and battalions of pikemen in the intervals between his cavalry wings— a strong contrast to the practice of his age, which was to place all the infantry in the centre and all the cavalry on the wings, each sustained only by itself. He quotes Montecuculi to the effect that: "In the armies of the ancients every regiment of foot had a certain proportion of horse and artillery . . . why therefore would they incorporate these distinct bodies together unless it was on account of the absolute necessity of such a connection . . ."

While scathing in his denunciation of those who merely accepted and continued, without test, the military customs of their forbears, Saxe was far from despising the storehouse of experience contained in history. But he went to it for principles and not for exact methods, and for that reason sought the best masters of all time, not merely the undigested surface parts of the immediate past. Like Ardant du Picq, the unheeded prophet of the 1870 disasters, he turned to the supreme military powers of ancient times for his research. It is curious that now, in 1927, some of the Staff Colleges are again rediscovering the wealth of military truth buried in the history of the ancient world, which was passed by in pre-war days in favour of an exclusive study of nineteenth-century campaigns.

Impressed with the wonderful adaptability and power of movement of the Roman organisa-tion—like finely tempered steel in its strength and flexibility,—Saxe derived his system from them. His infantry were to be formed into legions, each consisting of four regiments, and each regiment of four *centuries*, with a half-century of light infantry and a half-century of horse. The centuries were to be composed of ten " companies," each of fifteen men. With a view to combining economy in peace with a wisely directed expansion for war, Saxe formulated three distinct establishments. " In times of profound peace . . . the companies are only to consist of one sergeant, one corporal, and five veteran soldiers ; when preparations are making for a war that is expected, although not declared, an addition of five men must be made, and of ten when they are to be completed to full establishment. . . . The five veterans per company will constitute a fund for the occasional supply of officers and non-commissioned officers, by which means the inconvenience of making them of such as have never been in service will be avoided."

Thus in Saxe's " companies " we may see the germ of the modern infantry group, which, with its leader, his understudy, and little cluster of men, trained together in peace and held together amid the perils of the battlefield by the resulting bond of mutual understanding and reliance, is the base upon which are founded our new infantry tactics. The group was born of a quickened appreciation during the World War of the predominance of the moral factor, and the realisation that the kinship of the group and its feeling of mutual support fortified the spirit of the individual far better than the long, unnatural, and easily broken lines of pre-war practice.

If the Marshal's scheme is partially marred by the merging of the ten companies into four " maniples " for battle—a break in continuity of training, although a gain in power of control,—he was nearly two centuries ahead of his time in this idea of leaving intervals between the minor units of infantry.

Saxe, again, would hardly have committed the error that was made in organising the New Armies of 1914-15, for he says : " New raised regiments I am altogether averse to, *for unless they are grafted upon old ones*,[1] and commanded by good officers, eight or ten campaigns generally destroys them "—under modern conditions, 1915 showed that his estimate erred on the generous side.

Perhaps even more remarkable in its foresight and prophetic nature was another of his innovations. A practical inventor as well as a military philosopher—the two rôles are, curiously, often combined,—he produced in his

---

[1] The italics are the present author's.

" Amusettes " the prototype of the infantry accompanying guns, which has been a marked feature of recent post-war development. "Every century is furnished with a piece of ordnance of my own invention, called an *Amusette*, which carries above four thousand paces with extreme velocity . . . is drawn and worked with ease by two or three men, carries a half-pound ball, and is made with a convenience to hold a thousand, all which must render it of great service on numberless occasions in war." In further instructions upon their handling, Saxe says that the soldiers to work them are to be furnished from the century to which each belongs ; that before an engagement they are to be advanced in front along with the light troops; that "they can be fired two hundred times in an hour with ease " ; and that "upon occasion" the *Amusettes* of a regiment or legion can be massed for fire from an eminence or other commanding ground feature.

Thus, like the infantry guns of to-day, they were not a separate artillery arm, though their range was four times that of the ordinary field-piece of the time, and they were far more mobile than these cumbersome ox-drawn guns. Indeed, being man-handled, and with their crew of two, their half-pound ball, and high rate of fire, their tactics had some affinity with those of the machine-guns of the present.

A diagram shows them to have had a slender barrel about nine feet long, and a bore of two inches.

Other features of Saxe's "legion" were that the heavy as well as the light infantry were to have breech-loading arms; the men were to be furnished with bucklers of leather, prepared in vinegar—" they are not only of use to cover the arms, but whenever the troops are to engage standing, they may form a kind of parapet with them in an instant, by passing them from hand to hand along the front; two of them, the one upon the other, being musket-proof "— a further evidence of Saxe's appreciation of the value of armoured protection. He is, again, long in advance of his time when he condemns the " method of firing by word of command, as it detains the soldier in a constrained position, and prevents his aiming with any exactness." " How is it to be expected that they can, in such a position, retain an object in their eye till they receive the word to fire ? The most minute accident serves to discompose them . . . and their fire is in a large measure thrown away."

We see the origin of the *shoulder titles* worn by our troops to-day in the prescription that " the private soldiers are, moreover, to have a piece of brass fixed on each shoulder, with the number of the legion and regiment upon it to

which they belong, that they may at all times
be easily distinguished." The practice of the
eighteenth century was to name regiments after
their colonels; but the Marshal's understanding
of the moral factor is well shown by his dis-
approval of the custom on the ground that,
on a change of command, " the remembrance
of their former actions will then be apt to cease
together with that of their name." " It is much
easier to inspire a corps, which is distinguished
by a title peculiar to itself, with a spirit of
emulation." There is sound philosophy in his
subsequent remarks that " many persons, not
knowing why those regiments which bear the
names of provinces in France have always
behaved so particularly well, impute it altogether
to their natural courage, which is far from being
the real reason. . . . Thus we see that matters
of the utmost importance depend sometimes
on trifles which escape our notice."

The value of light infantry, so commonly
supposed to be a later development, was thoroughly understood by Saxe, who has dealt with
their tactics and equipment in great detail.
They were to be armed with a light fowling-
piece, breech-loading, and their accoutrements
to be of the lightest. They were to be exercised
constantly in jumping, running, and firing at
a mark at 300 paces distance, and the value of

competition was emphasised as an aid to the training. Their officers were to be chosen without regard to seniority and from the most active in the regiment.

In the assault, these light-armed foot were to be dispersed along the front of the regiment, opening fire when some three hundred paces from the enemy, and continuing to fire without word of command till within fifty paces, when they were to fall back within the intervals left, on the Roman plan, between the centuries— a notable innovation, these intervals, when regiments and even larger bodies normally advanced in a rigidly continuous line. Indeed, the idea of leaving intervals between units in a general attack had to wait until the last year of the World War for official acceptance! Yet such intervals were the only means of endowing the small infantry units with the power of manœuvre. While the light foot were thus skirmishing in front, the regiments would have doubled their ranks, and with the weight of their charge multiplied by their momentum, their shock would practically coincide with the cessation of the skirmishers' fire upon the enemy's harassed ranks—" disordered in a manner already by that floating and unevenness of the ranks which is unavoidable in the movement of . . . an extensive body."

Saxe calculated that there was little risk in
the innovation of leaving intervals in the front,
for not only would they be filled at the moment
of the shock by the light infantry, but the
enemy would be compelled to the hazardous
move of breaking up his own ranks if he
attempted to strike at the flanks of the centuries.
Then, directly the shock had succeeded and the
enemy broke in flight, the light infantry and
the horse were to be launched in pursuit, while
the centuries reformed, ready to receive them
back if repulsed or to renew the charge if
necessary.

Saxe also points out that by these tactics
his light infantry were too closely supported
by the centuries to be menaced by the enemy
horse, and that being trained marksmen firing
" at their own ease and discretion," their effect,
added to that of the *Amusettes*, would amply
compensate for the lack of the fire of the centuries, the serried ranks of which only impeded
their accuracy of aim. Saved from the dis-
turbance and delays of having to fire, the latter
would gain a supreme order and momentum
in their charge.

One other claim might be made for these
legions of the Marshal, that they contain the
embryo of the divisional system, the distribution
of the army into permanently organised divi-

sions capable of moving and acting independently, which in the Wars of the Revolution and of Napoleon revolutionised the conduct of war. If so, Saxe would live in history on this ground alone. That he realised in some measure the possibilities is clear, for he declares that " if the commander-in-chief of an army wishes . . . to obstruct the enemy in their projects, or, in short, to execute any of those various enterprises which are frequently found necessary in the course of a war, he has nothing more to do than to detach some particular legion upon it."

Having discussed in detail the " mechanism " of an army, the Marshal then turns to what he calls " the sublime branches of the art of war," and expounds, in a manner unfettered by custom and illuminated by a remarkable vision, how he would handle his overhauled and perfected machine—an army made up of these mobile and flexible legions. Space precludes a comprehensive account of his theories, for not content with platitude and airy generalisation, he takes a large number of imaginary or historical situations, shown on accompanying sketch-maps of pieces of ground, and explains the principles upon which he would act, and the methods he would employ in each case. On the subject of fortifications, their construction, attack and defence, he is distinguished equally by his in-

ventive powers and by his grasp of their restricted purpose—his mind transcends the limitations of that age of fortifications. The former
faculty enables him to produce schemes so
ingenious and yet so full of common-sense that,
as he claims, they "would not a little diminish
that rage for sieges which prevails at present."

His tactics for open warfare are instinct with
the idea of manœuvre, the embodiment of those
principles of surprise and of concentration *du
fort au faible* by which Napoleon at the end
of the century achieved his triumphs over
superior numbers. If Saxe, hampered by the
organic limitations of his time, fails to forecast
the application of these swift concentrations
and bold manœuvres to the wider fields of
strategy, his conceptions in the sphere of grand
tactics stamp him as the forerunner of the
great Corsican. In those days of parallel battle,
when the possibilities of manœuvre and concentration were almost untapped even by the
best captains of the age, Saxe's intellect towers
head and shoulders above his contemporaries.
Even the much-lauded oblique order of Frederick
the Great, which came to full bloom a decade
later, was but an insignificant step towards the
fulfilment of these principles that Saxe grasped
in their entirety. He clearly understood not
only the value of convergent attacks from two

directions simultaneously, but also the necessity
for fixing the enemy in front while manœuvring
to attack him in flank.   Saxe's manœuvres,
moreover, are not the mere extensions to over-
lap the enemy's front that were the best achieved
before the advent of Napoleon, but wide turning
movements to take the enemy's flank by surprise
or even to strike at his rear.   He is full, too, of
ruses, strategems, and feints to draw away the
enemy's reserves and distract his attention,
nor does he fear to weaken himself at one spot
in order to concentrate for a decisive blow
elsewhere.   He avoids the pitfalls which lie in
wait for the mere theorist, for every suggested
manœuvre is based on the nature of the ground,
and in an age of formality and artificial tactics
his appreciation of the terrain and its effect is
remarkable.   In introducing the subject, he
says : " It is the part of an able general to
derive advantages from every situation which
nature presents to him ; from plains, mountains, hollow ways, ponds, rivers, woods, and
an infinite number of other particulars, all of
which are capable of rendering great services
when they are converted to your purpose. . . ."
Among the actual examples which he cites,
his comments on Malplaquet are of interest to
students of English history.   He shows how the
Allies were so imprudent as to make dispositions

in which one-half of their force was totally separated from the other by a wood without any means of communication between, and he demonstrates how Marshal Villars might have concentrated against the left portion — with security, because the flanks and rear of the French army would have been under cover.

A shrewd comment further on is that " there is more address in making bad dispositions than is commonly imagined, provided they be such as are intentional, and so formed as to admit of being instantaneously converted into good ones : nothing can confound an enemy more, who has perhaps been anticipating a victory, than a stratagem of this kind ; for he perceives your weak spot, and disposes his army in a way to benefit the most from it ; but the attack is no sooner begun than he discovers the imposition . . . if he does not change his disposition he must infallibly be defeated, and the alternative, in the presence of his adversary, will be attended with the same fatal consequences."

The Marshal's use of redoubts, situated in front of his main striking force, to break up the enemy's attack and embarrass the pushing forward of reserves should the enemy press on without first capturing them, bears a distinct resemblance to the " pill-boxes " and strong

points which so hampered our advance at Ypres
in 1917. Equally significant is the disposition
of his batteries to fire obliquely to a flank instead
of direct to their front—for these intersecting
rays of fire across the front were one of the most
notable developments of the World War.

But there is one feature in which his ideas
are in strong contrast to those of 1915-17: like
the other great captains of history, he sought
always to turn the conditions to his advantage,
but when they were definitely adverse, he es-
chewed the vain attempt to press his attack in
spite of them. " A good opportunity for engaging should never be neglected merely because
the situation may not happen to be strictly
agreeable to your fancy, for you must form
your disposition according as you find the
situation, *and decline the attack altogether unless
you can make it with advantage. . . .*"

This view he develops still more strongly
when he discusses " the qualifications necessary
for the commander-in-chief of an army." He
sees clearly that pitched battles are only a
means to the end, and does not allow them
to obscure the real object—which is to subdue
the enemy country's will to resist. Here, certainly, he differs from Napoleon, who craved
for battle and sought it constantly. Opinions
will be divided as to the merits of these con-

trasting theories of war, but at least the sup-
porters of Saxe's view may point to the fact
that the end of his career left French power
intact and marked the zenith of Louis XV.'s
reign, while Napoleon's series of great battles
culminated in a France bankrupt of power and
with her manhood destroyed. If Saxe played
for smaller stakes, who shall say that the result
does not justify him ? He wrote : " I would
not be understood to say that an opportunity
of bringing on a general action, in which you
have all imaginable reason to expect victory,
ought to be neglected ; but only to insinuate
that it is possible to make war without trusting
anything to accident, which is the highest point
of skill and perfection within the province of
a general."

If, however, Saxe differed from the Napoleonic
conception of " absolute war," when he did take
up the dice of battle there were no half measures.
It has been said of Napoleon that he was the
first to develop the importance of pursuit and
to make it an essential factor, but Saxe had
preceded Napoleon in his grasp of the importance
of a relentless pursuit : " The maxim that it is
most prudent to suffer a defeated army to make
its retreat is . . . founded upon a false principle,
for you ought, on the contrary, to prosecute
your victory and to pursue your enemy to the

utmost of your power . . . his retreat will be
converted into a confirmed rout." He gives
the example of Ramillies, when the Allies were
gently pursuing the French army, retreating in
good order, until a single English squadron
approached and fired upon two French battalions,
and the commotion so alarmed the whole French
army that they broke up in hopeless confusion
and flight.

On the qualities necessary for a commander,
a few extracts from the Marshal will serve to
reveal his grasp of the gulf between the art of
command and the subordinate functions of
troop leadership.

" Of all the accomplishments that are required . . . courage is the first . . . the second
is genius, which must be strong and fertile in
expedients. The third is health." Yet at
Fontenoy, where Saxe had to be carried from
place to place in a wicker chariot, we see again,
as in the case of Nelson, the triumph of mind
and spirit over bodily infirmity. " He ought
to be mild in disposition; to be a stranger to
hatred; to punish without mercy, and especially
those who are the most dear to him, but never
through passion . . . His orders should be short
and simple . . . The generals under his command must be persons of very shallow parts
if they are at a loss how to perform the proper

manœuvre in consequence of this with their respective divisions. Then the commander-in-chief will have no occasion to embarrass or perplex himself; for if he takes upon him to do the duty of the sergeant of the battle, and to be everywhere in person, he will resemble the fly in the fable, which had the vanity to think itself capable of driving a coach." "I have seen very good colonels become very bad generals." "Many commanders-in-chief are no otherwise employed in a day of action than in making their troops march in a straight line, in seeing that they keep their proper distances . . . and in running about constantly . . . The reason of this defect is that very few officers study the grand detail, but spend all their time in exercising the troops, from a weak supposition that the military art consists alone in that branch; when therefore they arrive at the command of armies they are totally perplexed, and from their ignorance how to do what they ought, are very naturally led to do what they know." "The one of these branches, meaning discipline and the method of fighting, is methodical; the other is sublime; to conduct the latter of which, persons of ordinary abilities should by no means be appointed. Unless a man is born with talents for war, and those talents, moreover, are brought to perfection, it is impossible for him ever to be more than an indifferent general."

Another example of Saxe's breadth and depth of vision is seen when he foreshadows the modern Continental method of National Service, miscalled conscription. After pointing out the defects of the existing methods of quotas and pressgangs, he asks : " Would it not be much better to establish a law obliging men of all conditions of life to serve their king and country for the space of five years ? A law, which could not reasonably be objected to, as it is both natural and just for people to be engaged in the defence of that state of which they constitute a part ; and in choosing them between the years of twenty and thirty no inconvenience can be the result, for those are years devoted, as it were, to libertinism, which are spent in adventure and travel, and, in general, productive of but small comfort to parents . . . it would also create an inexhaustible fund of good recruits . . . In course of time every one would regard it as an honour rather than a duty to perform his task ; but to produce this effect upon a people it is necessary that no sort of distinction should be admitted, no rank or degree excluded . . . If we take a survey of all nations, what a spectacle do they present ? We behold some men rich, indolent, and voluptuous, whose happiness is produced by a multitude of others, who are employed in flattering their passions . . . the assemblage of these distinct classes of men, oppressors and oppressed, forms what is called society; the refuse of which is collected to compose the soldiery; but such measures and such men are far different from those by means of which the Romans conquered the universe."

Later, speaking of the Army as a career, he insists on the necessity of paying officers adequately and giving to all hope of advancement, "because a man who devotes himself to the service should look upon it as an entrance into some religious order; he should neither have nor acknowledge any other home than that of his regiment, and at the same time, whatever position he may be in, should esteem himself honoured by it . . ."

Not only on the raising of troops is he curiously modern in outlook, but also on the prevention of wastage through disease—a subject almost neglected until after the Boer War. Quoting some of the appalling figures of wastage, he says: "I could produce many instances . . . which can only be imputed to the change of climate; but the use of vinegar was the grand secret by which the Romans preserved their armies . . . this is a fact that few perhaps

have attended to, but which is of very great
importance to all commanders who have a
regard for their troops, and any ambition to
conquer their enemies. . . . The Romans distributed it by order amongst the men, every
one receiving a sufficient quantity to serve him
for several days, and pouring a few drops of it
into the water which he drank."

From a multitude of other ideas we must at
least quote one of historical interest, which
concerns the origin of martial music and of the
term " tactics."

" Almost every military man makes use of
the word *tactick*, and takes it for granted that
it means the art of drawing up an army in order
of battle ; yet not one can properly say what
the ancients understood by it. It is universally
a custom . . . to beat a *march*, without knowing
the original or true use of it, and as universally
believed that the sound is intended for nothing
more than a warlike ornament. Yet sure we
ought to entertain a better opinion of the Greeks
and Romans . . . for it is absurd to imagine
that martial sounds were invented by them for
no other purpose than to confound their senses.

" If on a march the front is ordered to quicken
its pace, the rear must unavoidably lose ground
before it can perceive it ; to regain which it
sets up a run . . . which presently throws the

whole into disorder. . . . The way to obviate these inconveniences . . . is very simple, because it is dictated by nature; it is nothing more than to march in *cadence,* in which alone consists the whole mystery, and which answers to the military pace of the Romans. . . . It was to preserve this that martial sounds were first invented, and drums introduced; and in this sense only is to be understood the word *tactick* . . . by means of this you will always be able to regulate your pace at pleasure . . . and the whole will step with the same foot. . . . Nothing is so common as to see a number of persons dance together during a whole night, even with pleasure; but, deprive them of music, and the most indefatigable will not be able to bear it for two hours, which sufficiently proves that sounds have a secret power over us, disposing our organs to bodily exercise, and deluding, as it were, the toil of them."

The conclusion of the book is worthy of the original and unconventional outlook of the man, for, in his own words: "After treating of a science which furnishes us with means for the destruction of the human race, I am now going to propose methods towards facilitating the propagation of it."

His concern over the declining birth-rate of France has a strikingly modern ring about it,

and his suggestions, and the scandal they caused
in his day, both find parallels in our own post-
war era. " I am persuaded there will one day
be an absolute necessity to make some altera-
tion in our religion with regard to this, for if
one considers how many institutions it establishes
which are an hindrance to propagation, this
diminution of the species will no longer be so
surprising. The frequency of marriage is much
prevented by it, and the flower of a woman's
youth is often spent in waiting for a husband.
. . . A legislator who would form a system on
propagation . . . would lay the foundation of
a monarchy that could not fail of becoming
one day formidable to the whole world.   He
ought, in the first place, to eradicate debauchery,
which, so far from being dictated by nature,
is one of her most inveterate enemies ; it would
be necessary, therefore, to inculcate by education
that sterility is one infallible consequence of it,
which, after the age of fifteen, should be
accounted dishonourable ; and that the more
children a woman had the happier would be her
situation," which Saxe proposed to encourage
by a system of tithes and motherhood endow-
ments. " But the most effectual means would
be by establishing a law that no future marriage
should endure for more than five years, or be
renewable without a dispensation, in case there

was no child born in that time. . . . That such
parties likewise, as should have renewed their
marriage three times and have had children,
should be afterwards inseparable. All the
theologians in the world would not be able to
prove any impiety in this system, because
marriage was instituted by divine authority
on no other account but that of propagation."
He then advocates women's right to freedom
of choice, and argues that this liberty and the
system of limited marriages would eradicate
debauchery.

The best comment on these ideas is supplied
by the editor of the memoirs, who, admitting
that they proceed from a good intention, says :
" I believe all the world will agree with me that
the Marshal was a greater general than he was
a civilian; and that these limited marriages,
instead of doing good, would, on the contrary,
make a dreadful confusion amongst society;
for how many children, void of both fortune
and education, would be abandoned by the
caprice of their parents ? " " This liberty, moreover, of separation after marriage is of very
little consequence with regard to propagation;
for it is no more than what is secretly practised
in these times, although it may lack the sanction
of a law to confirm it. If mankind diminishes
in numbers, let us not attribute it to the fetters

of marriage, for, alas ! there is nothing to which we nowadays make ourselves slaves so little as to conjugal fidelity." The editor then puts forward his own theory that the enemy to propagation is "luxury ; formerly it was confined to the palaces of the great, but now it prevails even in cottages, and it is that which multiplies our wants, and renders children a burden to their parents, because their maintenance and education become thereby attended with extraordinary expenses. We were much happier in those times when plainness and frugality were not accounted dishonourable."

III.

GUSTAVUS ADOLPHUS—FOUNDER OF MODERN WAR

III.

GUSTAVUS ADOLPHUS—FOUNDER OF MODERN WAR.

LET any one speak of the Great Captains, and Gustavus Adolphus is almost certain to be enumerated in the list, yet he is, strangely enough, little more than a name to many British students of war and military history for whom the campaigns of Marlborough, Frederick, Napoleon, Lee among the moderns, or Alexander, Hannibal, and Cæsar among the ancients, are familiar ground.

Considering that he stands on the threshold of the modern world, with the dark shadows of mediævalism behind and the triumphant vista of the unchained mind in front, and that if we seek a starting point for a history of warfare in modern times, he is the first eminent figure we can find, the dearth of military studies of him in this country is remarkable, the more so that the epoch of transition in which he lived is so well known and widely studied in its political and religious aspects.

With Gustavus's contribution to the cause of

religious liberty in Europe and his political influence on the formation of modern Europe we are not concerned here, our object being to assess his effect on the art and science of war, and, stripping his memory alike of the pall of ignorance and the tinsel of legend, to bring into the light both his qualities and his limitations as a soldier.   These limitations, be it understood, were mainly those of his age, and the interest to us is to discover how far he overcame them, and in doing so advanced the art of war beyond the stage at which he found it.

It is by the progress achieved, not the incompleteness of the task, that we should judge such a man, taking into account particularly the tools he had to work with, and upon what extent of foundation he had to build.   Higher credit, and that rightly so, is normally accorded to the pioneer, the originator, no matter how primitive his creation may appear to sophisticated modern eyes, than to his successors, who simply improve and develop the initial product. " But," it may be said, " the art of war was not an invention of Gustavus.   Behind him he had the experience and developments of two thousand years of recorded warfare, and therefore should he not be judged by the standard of earlier great captains, of Alexander, Hannibal, or Scipio even ? "

At first glance there would appear some justice in this view, for the Renaissance and the impetus given to classical studies undoubtedly brought within his reach the military wisdom of the ancients, an advantage lacked by the mediæval generals, and one which we know that Gustavus had made use of during his youth. Moreover, by this test only the purblind admirer of the great Swede would pretend that he was the equal of those mentioned above, even less perhaps of such strategists as the Mongols, Jenghiz Khan and Sabutai.

But just as the Renaissance and the Reformation form in civil history the portals of the modern world, so in military history does the development of firearms. With these a new factor was introduced into warfare which, if it did not change its foundations, almost completely demolished its superstructure.

Though firearms had been increasing in importance for generations before his time, it was left for Gustavus to build up the walls of the modern art of war on the unchanging foundation principles, and in a way adapted to the new conditions brought about by fire. In this lies his claim to eternal fame, and by this test that as a pioneer he must primarily be judged.

Born in December 1594, six years after England's great blow for the cause of liberty against

the Armada, the future defender of Protestantism
in Northern Europe came of a lineage that
promised heroic qualities. His grandfather, the
great Gustavus Vasa, had not only thrown off
the yokes of Denmark and the papacy and established the Vasa dynasty, but had raised the
Swedes from being a semi-barbarous people,
who, in his own words, were so short-sighted as
to rob every merchant who ventured among them.

The development of the new kingdom went
on under his successors, who, if they warred
among themselves, were men born to leadership and of high culture. Intellect was indeed
the birthright of the Vasas, marked also with
a strain of insanity which, proverbially, is akin
to genius—the happy form it took in the case
of the second Gustavus.

For his future rôle his upbringing was ideal,
politics, literature, military science, and physical
development being wisely blended in his education under the tuition of able instructors and
the careful direction of his father, who imparted
a strong religious impulse. To those who appreciate Xenophon's ' Cyropædia ' as perhaps the
greatest of all military text-books, it is of special
significance that Xenophon was one of his
favourite authors, and that Gustavus himself
declared later that he knew of " no writer better
than he for a true military historian."

But fortune placed in Gustavus's way the opportunity to combine practice with theory even during his formative years. Sigismund, the Catholic King of Poland, still strove to regain the throne of Sweden that he had held and lost; Denmark dreamt of a reunited Scandinavia under her sway, and, holding Norway and the keys of the Baltic, was a constant menace to Swedish independence; while Russia, though a minor Power, was even then a thorn in Sweden's side. War between these countries was recurrent, and thus in the hard school of reality the military ability of Gustavus was forged and his character developed. At the early age of sixteen he was given a small command in the Danish war, and distinguished himself by the surprise night capture of the fortress of Christianopel. Later that same year, 1611, the death of Charles IX. brought Gustavus to the throne—no cheerful prospect for a youth to face, with three enemies at the gates and the parlous finances of his country tying his hands. If ever in the world's history, it was youth's trial and opportunity— his rôle not simply to take over a brilliant heritage, but, instead, a bankrupt concern, and his achievement not merely to restore its stability, but carry it to heights of influence and power beyond youth's wildest dreams. More striking still was that instead of counsellors of ripe age and experience, the young King chose as his chief minister Axel Oxenstierna, prudent and calm beyond his years, it is true, but nevertheless only eleven years older than Gustavus. For Sweden and the world the partnership was a happy one, their qualities so different as to be complementary, and knit by a bond of friendship rare in the relations of kings and subjects.

The immediate problem was the danger from Denmark, and in this early stage of his career Gustavus was handicapped by the inertness and incapacity of his chief officers, until he was able to replace them by that brilliant band of young generals, trained and advanced to high command by him, who figured so prominently in his later campaigns and after his untimely death at Lützen. But when the clouds loomed blackest, the rally of the Swedish peasantry on behalf of King and country staved off the menace, and, though disappointed of military success, Gustavus obtained a peace by negotiation greatly to his advantage. The fortresses of Calmar on the Baltic and Elfsborg on the North Sea, the two sea keys of his kingdom on the east and west, were yielded to him partly as the fruit of his stubborn resistance and partly by payment, money difficult to afford and yet assuredly well spent in this case.

With Denmark out of the way, Gustavus

next prepared to deal with Russia, and after a somewhat desultory war, the peace of 1617 obtained for Sweden the provinces of Ingria and Carelia, including the site of present Petrograd—the real importance of this accession of territory being that Russia was shut out from the Baltic, so effectively securing Gustavus's communications for his later wars.

Poland only remained, and a long truce till 1621 gave Gustavus the chance to begin the organisation of his " new model " army, and so far as possible the resources of his kingdom, as well as to widen his horizon by travel. Undertaken incognito as Captain Gars (Gustavus Adolphus Rex Sueciae), these tours through Germany gave him the better chance to acquaint himself with the people with whom he was to be allied and the country he was to fight over in the coming years. At home these years were also his main period of civil and legal change and organisation, during which he altered the policy of his predecessors, restoring the power of the nobility but widening its bounds by the inclusion of all who rendered service to the State, making it a nobility of merit rather than purely of birth. Above all, he gave it a military orientation, the officers of the army taking their share in the Diets, and so created a military monarchy in which the hereditary nobles, purged of their selfish elements, and the leaders of the army were fused into a solid buttress for the royal power.

Over this new policy controversy raged hotly, the protagonists being Oxenstierna on the one hand, and Gustavus's old tutor, John Skytte, on the other, who wished Gustavus to finish his father's work of crushing out the nobility. But the ideas of Axel Oxenstierna prevailed, though largely because Gustavus himself inclined to the latter's views. "If Oxenstierna, by his large wisdom, his astuteness and tact, often proved himself the brain of the duality, it is certain that Gustavus was the directing will and the executive hand."

The names of the two are indissolubly linked in the records of the age, and the minister-general normally acts the part of a brake on the King's ambitions and sometimes over-bold schemes. Yet though Oxenstierna stood essentially for prudence, it was no merely negative quality, and in some of the strategical turning points of the German campaigns, his was the more daring attitude and perhaps the longer vision. Though always the most trusted counsellor of Gustavus, his influence was less decisive in the later years, and one of the great questions of history is whether the Imperial Power would not have been broken completely and the course of the world's history changed had Oxenstierna's bold strategical advice prevailed after Breitenfeld.

With these domestic changes the Polish wars interfered little, for, though continuing inter-mittently until 1629, they were punctuated by frequent periods of truce. Space forbids a detailed account of their course, nor, because of their relative indecisiveness, are they of great historical interest, save as the training ground of Gustavus and his army. Unhappily, even for this purpose, the tactical details are wanting. The war correspondent had yet to make his appearance, and such few of Gustavus's de-spatches as survived the great fire at Stockholm Castle in 1697 are laconic to a degree, dismissing in a few lines a siege or engagement that cost a thousand or more lives.

Of the deeply interesting process by which the weapon of his military triumphs was forged hardly any record exists. We learn that at Walhof, his first pitched battle, by a rapid night march " with a detachment of cavalry and a thousand musketeers " he aimed to strike a Polish force of 7000 under Sapieha before Radziwil's force could join the latter ; that when the rival forces drew up for battle, Gus-tavus, sighting some disorder among the enemy's troops, placed his musketeers to support his attack with fire, and then charged in and routed the enemy with his cavalry. From these meagre details we gleam perhaps the earliest example in modern history of the principles of *concentration*, both strategical and tactical, and of the combination of *fire and movement*, which forms the burden of every military manual nowadays.

It is by such slight hints that we are able to follow the steady progress of the King's generalship, as well as the mobility and hitting power of his army.

When the war finally terminated in 1629 by a six years' truce, it was not through decisive victory, though Sweden's success had been sufficient to bring her considerable gains of territory, but because of Sigismund's recognition that his prospects were dwindling, combined with the influence of the French and English ambassadors. Gustavus was wanted on a greater stage, and Richelieu's master mind pulled the strings to release him for the new part.

The Thirty Years' War had begun in 1618, but though frequent appeals had been made to Gustavus to throw his weight in the scales on behalf of his brother Protestants in Germany, Gustavus refused to commit himself to an adventure of such magnitude until he was quit of the Russian and Polish dangers, his command of the Baltic secure, and his forces trained and ready for the supreme trial of strength, and, above all, unless he could feel sure of adequate support from outside and the genuine co-operation of the threatened Protestant states of Germany themselves.

In 1624, when the full meaning of the tide of Imperial triumph was gauged by the other Powers, England, France, and Holland, fearful of the aggrandisement of Austria and her combination with Spain, sought eagerly to offset the menace by bringing some new champion into the German arena. England took the first hand in the game, influenced by the fact that she was the " keep " of the reformed faith, and also because the ill-fated Frederick, chased summarily from his Bohemian throne and Palatine dominions, was the son-in-law of James I. Two English ambassadors, Robert Anstruther and James Spens, visited both Christian of Denmark and Gustavus of Sweden. But the latter had no intention of being made a cat's-paw, and to the overtures replied : " If any one thinks it easy to make war upon the most powerful potentate in Europe, and upon one, too, who has the support of Spain and so many of the German princes . . . and if he think, also, it easy to bring into common action so many minds, each having in view their own separate object . . . we shall be quite willing to leave to him the glory of his achievements and all its accompanying advantages."

Christian of Denmark proved more complaisant —and less far-sighted in estimating the difficulties—with results that were soon disastrous. His army and generals unequal to the task, and England proving a broken reed on which to rely even for financial support, Christian was defeated, thrown out of Germany, and compelled to sue for peace. With all Germany overrun by his armies, the Emperor followed up his military and political triumph by the famous Edict of Restitution of May 1629, by which all the bishoprics, churches, and church property acquired by the Protestants since 1552 were torn from them and restored to the Catholics, an act, moreover, carried out in the most ruthless manner.

Then while all Germany groaned under the tyranny of the Emperor and the barbarism of the Imperial armies, Richelieu, politician before Catholic prelate, fearing the Imperial ambitions, made his bid to secure Gustavus as a counterpoise.

His hands at last free, his forces prepared for the great stake, and his religious sentiments spurring him on, Gustavus was now willing to listen to advances. Above all, he appreciated the danger to Sweden of an Imperial hold on the Baltic. He had already sought to guard against this last menace by aiding the citizens of Stralsund, the noted Baltic port, in their resistance to Wallenstein, which proved the one real check to the Imperial general's all-conquering progress.

In a letter to Oxenstierna in 1628, Gustavus had uttered the prophetic truth, which later history has made so clear, "that the wars that are made in Europe are complicated, and nearly always become general," one of many indications that he had long realised his entry into the struggle to be inevitable.

But for a time he hesitated as to the choice, "ought he to take the offensive or defensive in the war." Oxenstierna supported the latter view, but Gustavus here took the bolder course, arguing the danger that would arise from an Imperial fleet in the Baltic : " If one tries not to take his ports by land forces, I see not the means of long defending the kingdom. It would not be well to transport into Sweden the seat of war, for we are never more feeble than in our own country. You know the extent of our coasts and the number of ports we have to defend. I am in accord with you, that it is scarcely possible to make war in Germany; nevertheless, if we gain the advantage, I do not believe we shall be so poor that we cannot

have some advantage. . . . We cannot take
away a strong army because it is necessary to
keep many infantry in Sweden to observe Denmark. It will be necessary then to employ
especially foreigners. We think, however, to
put in campaign fifteen thousand foot and
nine thousand horse. And though you object
to the feebleness of our army and the force of
the two armies of the enemy, you should consider that he has an extensive country to
occupy, and many cities to guard, which requires a large number of troops. It is not well
to lose sight that the power of the enemy is
more in fame than in the reality, and that the
loss of a single pitched battle would render his
position very critical "—an inspired forecast that
Breitenfeld was to prove true. If Gustavus,
unlike his rival Wallenstein, had no recourse
to astrology in order to foresee the future, he
was gifted with a remarkable measure of foresight, amounting almost to second sight, as to
the course both of his military fortunes and
himself. Was he vouchsafed a vision of the
tragic day of Lützen, when in his parting address
to the Diet he said : " As to what concerns
me, I am not unaware of the danger to which
I expose myself. Already many times my
blood has flowed for Sweden, and my love for
the country doubtless will cost my life some

day; for it is by being often carried to the well that the pitcher is finally broken."

The die was soon cast; on 4th July 1630, exactly one hundred years after the Confession of Augsburg was published, Gustavus, the new champion of Protestantism, landed in Germany —on the island of Usedom, near the mouth of the Oder, the great river round which his earlier campaigns were to centre.

At the news Ferdinand, swollen with triumph, is said to have remarked, "so we have another little enemy," and his flattering courtiers made jest, "The snow-king will melt as he approaches the Southern Sun." Fortune favoured the bold throw, for it was at this juncture that Wallenstein was dismissed from his command at the instigation of the German Catholic princes, who resented his arrogance and power, and made the excuse of his army's exactions. In this successful interference they were substantially aided not only by the Court of Madrid, but by the subtler intrigues of Richelieu, who, negotiating at that time his secret treaty with Gustavus, wished to clear the path for his new counterpoise to the Imperial power. His envoy, the Capuchin friar, Father Joseph, artfully urged on the Emperor that "It would be well to oblige the electors in this trifling matter; it will help to secure the Roman crown for the

King of Hungary, and when the storm shall
have passed away, Wallenstein will be ready
enough to resume his former station." Gaining
his end in this vital matter, Father Joseph
proceeded to ensure that the Imperial plans
were upset over the King of Hungary's election.
Bitterly the Emperor declared " a worthless
friar has disarmed me with his rosary, and
put six electoral hats into his narrow cowl."
Had he foreseen the future, how much greater
would his chagrin have been ? For not only
did he lose the service of his best general during
what was the critical early period of Gustavus's
invasion, when the scales trembled in the
balance, but with Wallenstein disappeared the
greater part of his army, raised by personal
contract as was the custom of the time, and
so not bound by any ties of patriotism. Many
of them indeed enlisted under the banner of
Gustavus.

It is difficult to overestimate the influence
this tremendous weakening of the Imperial army
exercised on the fortunes of the war, and of
Europe, allowing the Swedish King to consolidate his position in Germany and widen his
base for the far-reaching operations of the next
year.

But when Gustavus took his momentous decision he had no conception of this huge stroke

of luck in store. All that he could see was
the Imperial power bestriding Germany like a
Colossus, the Protestant States beaten to their
knees, so cowed indeed by adversity and the
merciless devastations of the Imperial armies,
that when Gustavus landed, not a prince,
not a city, dared to give a welcome to the
champion they had summoned. So reduced
was their courage, so slender their hope, that
all waited to see how his venture would fare
before committing themselves to his support—
silent awe-stricken spectators of another David
and Goliath duel.

Strange how the story of the Great Captains
repeats itself : Alexander setting out for Asia
to attack the vast Persian empire and its armed
millions, Hannibal crossing the Alps to challenge the Roman power at its seat, were not
more daring than this seeming gambler's throw
by Gustavus with the odds so heavily against
him.

II.

Here on the threshold of his German campaigns it is a fitting juncture to analyse the
character and the forces of Gustavus, to discover what manner of man was this audacious
champion of Protestantism, and what were the

military factors on which he relied to counter-
balance the Emperor's vast superiority in men
and resources.   In this study we are concerned
essentially with Gustavus as a soldier; our
object is to assess his calibre as an artist and
scientist of war and his contribution to military
progress.   Since history shows us that his
dramatic successes were due rather to the new
pattern instrument of war he created than to
any revolutionary developments in strategy, as
was the case with Napoleon, or even in tactics,
we are justified in devoting the major part of
our space to this question.

First, of the man, for thereby we gain the
clue to his influence on warfare and the course
of his military methods and reforms.

In person tall and well-formed, becoming
stout in these later years—though but thirty-
eight at his death,—of ruddy complexion, blue
eyes, bright yellow hair, his Viking blood mani-
fested itself both in his looks and his actions.
Foreigners bestowed on him the name of " the
golden King of the North."   In disposition and
manner frank, generous, with a marked courtesy
and dignity of bearing, though subject to occasional fierce gusts of temper.   With a strong
sense of what was due to his royal position,
he was yet remarkably easy of access and genial,
and with personal magnetism added to constant

acts of spontaneous kindness, it was little
wonder that he won the adoration of his troops;
while his humane conduct in war, far beyond
his age, compelled the respect of his bitterest
foes.   In personal valour, carried to the pitch
of recklessness, he surpasses even Alexander in
the rôle of the great captains, and where the
King led the way into the danger zone so impetuously, how could his troops but be inspired
to heroic feats?   Surveying the upshot in
history, and remembering what vast issues rested
on his life, we may regret that his fiery courage
was not tempered, but instinct conquers reason
and compels our admiration.   "Lion of the
North" indeed, the men of his time aptly
characterised the man and his achievements.

Thirteen times wounded in his earlier
campaigns, his personal daring had its spring
in more than mere love of danger.   To the
envoy of Holland who remonstrated with him,
suggesting that it would suffice to trace the
plan and leave its execution to others, Gustavus replied: "One cannot take cities by
marking circles on a table in his chamber.   When
the schoolmaster is absent, the scholars put
aside their books."

Again, another reason in the remarks of the
Scottish officer, Monro, who was in the service
of Gustavus: "The lack of good charts *and the*

*great importance which he attached to knowledge
of the ground,* caused him to reconnoitre in
person and expose himself very near to danger,
for he was short-sighted." In present days
when the vital importance of personal reconnaissance is stressed throughout all armies, this
ray from the past throws light on one claim of
Gustavus to be the founder of modern war.

An incident which also illuminates his military
character is that narrow escape at the siege of
Demmin when, on such a reconnaissance, he
was caught leg-deep in a marsh, the ice breaking, and in his predicament came under a heavy
fire. Reproached by Captain Dumaine, a Scot,
for thus risking his precious life, Gustavus
genially acknowledged his imprudence, but
added: "It is my nature not to believe well
done except what I do myself: it is also necessary that I see everything by my own eyes."

From Monro we get many such sidelights:
"I serve with great pleasure such a general,
and I could find with difficulty a similar man,
who was accustomed to be the first and the
last where there is danger ; who gained the
love of his officers by the part he took in their
troubles and fatigues ; who knew so well how
to trace the rules of conduct for his warriors
according to times and circumstances ; . . . who
divined the projects and knew the resources of

his enemies, their plans, their forces, their discipline, likewise the nature and position of the places which they occupied "—such an epitome of the principles of leadership would make a model basis for an address to young officers to-day.

Unlike some modern commanders, however, he placed efficiency beyond friendship, nor would he tolerate stupid officers because of their social gifts, or on the ground that they were "good fellows." On this point Monro tells us, " He did not like the officers who lacked intelligence, and he never left one without being assured that his orders were understood,"—how pertinent the phrase sounds. " He arrested an officer who, while the fortifications of Stettin were being repaired, stated that the earth was frozen. In affairs which had relation to the needs of war he did not admit of excuses."

There is sound military psychology, as well as a flavour of the World War, in the comment, " When he was weakest he digged the most in the ground; and this he did, not only to secure his soldiers from the enemy, but also to keep them from idleness."

But in nothing is his claim to be the forerunner of modern doctrine more marked than in his emphasis on *information, inter-communication,* and *co-operation.*

To this his correspondence and orders bear witness; every time in the instructions sent to his subordinate commanders he reiterates not only that they are to keep him informed of the situation, but also to get in touch and keep in touch with the commanders of neighbouring detachments. For example, at the end of instructions to Horn, dated 30th March 1630—"Do not fail to inform us of what happens in the district, also of all that comes to your knowledge about the enemy's situation; above all, don't neglect to keep up a daily correspondence with Kagge. . . ." Here, again, is an instruction of 18th February to Bauer, which is an excellent example of the principles of security and economy of force—"The King always insists that general officers must keep up correspondence between themselves. If the enemy, with only a part of his troops, attempts an invasion in a particular quarter, the dispositions must be regulated accordingly, and the forces to oppose him proportioned to his numbers, ensuring above all that the crossings of the Reckiwitz, Tribal, and Tollensee are well held. These rivers serve as entrenchments and sure means of easy communication. The rest of the troops will remain in their quarters at least until there is an urgent need of them to join those detailed to act against the enemy."

Gustavus's orders are a model of which a modern staff officer might be proud, the paragraphs numbered, each short, crisp, and embodying one specific point; the whole in a logical sequence that is reminiscent of modern practice—information as to the enemy, intention of the commander, and method of execution first, then administrative arrangements, and finally inter-communication.

Perhaps the most notable feature of his instructions, the hallmark of the Great Captain who foresees all contingencies and prepares for all emergencies, is the way Gustavus indicates the various moves open to the enemy, and the action to be taken in each case.

If in his strategy, as we shall show, his fulfilment of the principles of direction and surprise was less convincing than that of security — of which he may truly be said to be the father in modern war,—he at least realised the value of mobility and of concentration *du fort au faible*, to a degree markedly ahead of his times.

Here is a typical message to Horn in July 1631 : " We have already made clear to you our wish that you should come here without delay with your troops ; we repeat it again, because there could not be a better chance, to all appearances, to administer a check to the enemy, provided that you are not late in

arriving. Do all that you can then to get here
as soon as possible, so that we can profit by
this splendid chance before the enemy can be
reinforced."

In another of the same month we find a deft
combination of reproof and encouragement:
" We learn with surprise that instead of sending
to Old Brandenburg a thousand well-trained
and disciplined men, to guarantee this place
against enemy attack, you have ordered there
the recruits of Colonel Berch and three hundred
Swedish soldiers also recruits, and all undis-
ciplined. As we learn that the enemy is not
advancing towards Brandenburg and Spandow,
although he is camped near the river, where
he can easily build a bridge, we wish you to
carry out our instructions to the letter, which
are that you should choose a thousand good
musketeers from your army, of whom you will
send three hundred to reinforce the garrison
of Spandow, and the other seven hundred to
Brandenburg. With the surplus, as the issue
of our plans, *and the moment of acting with
success*, depends entirely on your prompt arrival,
you will make the greatest speed to join us.
If you ever attach some value to rendering us
a service that we appreciate, this, which is
urgent and helpful, will earn you a right to our
regard.

" *P.S.*—Move the troops in as open formation as possible during your march in order to travel faster—which is the supreme requirement. . . . It does not matter if the artillery pieces follow after you, provided that you arrive with the troops."

But modern though Gustavus is in many respects, it is not to be expected that he should be entirely emancipated from the toils of mediævalism, where war was treated as a glorified joust instead of a sharp and decisive life and death struggle between nations—hedged in by formal observances and other relics of chivalry that are now the characteristic of the duel, and discarded in real fighting. Thus on the field of Breitenfeld we find Gustavus, conforming to old custom, sending a trumpeter to challenge Tilly and his army before battle is joined. Indeed, more than a century beyond Gustavus, after such great captains as Turenne, Condé, Montecuculi, Eugene, and Marlborough had all made their contribution to the art of war, we find the immortal comedy of Fontenoy : " Gentlemen of France, fire first."

Picturesque and redolent of a stately courtesy, but hopelessly impractical, the incident appeals to our emotions as much as it is condemned by our reason.

From the man himself let us turn to his

instrument, and it is here in the organisation
of his army and his military reforms that Gustavus's modern trend of thought finds its fullest
expression.

If he was not the inventor of the modern
standing army, he was at least the first to
develop it systematically, to place it on a rational
basis, in fact the pioneer in building up a true
regular army and national military organisation—he may well be called the father of the
present European system of conscription.

In the Middle Ages the military forces were
either of the feudal or militia type, who turned
out for a short period and returned to their
homes on its expiry, or else mercenary bands
who hired themselves out to any ruler, irrespec-
tive of nationality, who was willing to pay
them. Regular soldiers only in the sense that
they made war their profession, they were
the best troops of their age, but unreliable
and naturally averse to vigorous action—where
decisive victory would remove the need of their
services and so throw them out of employment.

But despite this drawback, from the collapse
of feudalism onwards their importance steadily
and inevitably increased, and in the sixteenth
and seventeenth centuries the soldier of fortune
was the dominant feature in warfare. Until,
and apart from Gustavus, such embryo standing

armies as existed were but an enlarged species of royal bodyguard.

Working to some extent on a foundation laid by the earlier Vasa kings, Gustavus created a national army, raised, paid, fed and equipped by the State, with a militia behind it for home defence, which also supplied drafts to the regular forces.

In numerous books the statement is made that Gustavus's armies were raised on a system of land tenure, but a study of the records of the time shows that the " Indelning," peculiar to Sweden, did not uniformly take this form, despite the King's efforts.

The orders issued for the Kingdom in 1627 bear on this point, and are vividly reminiscent of some features of our World War experience: "The peasants are to be convoked by districts; the summons being given from the pulpits by the pastors, with the exhortation for every man to attend. . . . The pastors shall first . . . make out a list of all the male inhabitants of fifteen years and upwards, for the correctness of which they are held responsible. The justices and bailiffs of the districts shall see that this is faithfully done by the parish clergy. . . . A jury of twelve men shall be formed, the same who sit at the ting—or district court. With the assistance of this jury, the

royal commissioners are to cause the assembled
men to be divided into groups or lists of ten
each. *These are arranged not according to the
number of farms or landed estates, but by the
count of heads.*[1] In conducting the conscription,
care is to be exercised that he who is taken
for military service from every group shall be
fresh and sound, strong of limb, and, so far
as can be ascertained, courageous; in years,
from eighteen to thirty. It is provided that
where there are servants in the group they
shall be taken before the peasants, yet so that
the son of parents who already have one son
in the service, or have lost one in battle, shall
be spared. . . . The situation of the farms
shall also be considered, so that he who possesses
a large farm may have the preference of being
spared in the selection made. . . ." From this
conscription no one was exempt, save the house
and farm servants of the nobles—though not
their retainers—and of the clergy. But essential
services, transport and munitions, were safe-
guarded as in recent days and treated as " reserved occupations " by the rule that in mines,
saltpetre works, munition factories and ship-
wharves, only superfluous hands were liable for
conscription.

Again, the presence of the jury gave the

---

[1] The italics are the present writer's.

conscription a democratic flavour, and anything done in its absence was illegal.

Oxenstierna provides further information on the system, as well as an amusing sidelight: " When King Gustavus Adolphus set about the great Prussian war, conscription was voted according to the number of heads, and the crown obtained in the first years . . . fifteen thousand; . . . but afterwards, when every man had time to think of some evasion, not more than six or seven thousand. Conscription by this count of heads was the old custom, and the King vainly endeavoured to persuade the people to allow it to be made by the number of farms, so that one soldier might be furnished by a certain number of peasants, by an arrangement among themselves."

These conscriptions were for the infantry, from which the nobles were exempt—every noble was held liable for service in the cavalry.

In addition, however, to the conscripted troops, a proportion were raised by voluntary enlistment, mainly for the cavalry. In the infantry the enlisted troops were generally foreigners, at first individual enlistments, but later, as Gustavus's needs grew and his Swedish resources of man-power waned, by whole regiments. In his final German campaigns the percentage of foreigners was very high, comprising half his infantry ; we have mentioned the disbanded troops of Wallenstein, and prisoners of war constantly changed sides as the price of freedom. But no contingents figure more prominently in the history of his wars than the Scottish, who at Breitenfeld provided no less than three brigades, while such names as Hepburn, Ramsay, Monro, Leslie, and many another Scottish captain are indissolubly linked with the victories of Gustavus. In Gustavus's third campaign, of British alone, mainly Scots, there were 6 generals, 30 colonels, 51 lieutenant-colonels, and 10,000 men. It is an interesting coincidence that in the storm of Frankfort on the Oder, where the Scots took a foremost part in the assault, the last stand of the Imperialists was made by a body of Irish under Colonel Walter Butler.

By these various means Gustavus formed early in 1630 an army of 76,000 men, of whom 43,000 were Swedes, but of this total only 13,000 landed with him in Germany, while David Leslie occupied Stralsund and Rügen with another 6000—a desperately slender force for so gigantic a venture, though another 25,000 came to him as reinforcements before the end of the year. Of the surplus, 16,000 were left to garrison Sweden, and three contingents of from 5000 to 7000 apiece in Finland,

the Baltic provinces, and Prussia.   As the
armies of Wallenstein and Tilly totalled over a
100,000 in Germany, we may appreciate how
fortunate   for   Gustavus   was   the   former's
dismissal.

But heterogeneous as was the Swedish army
in race, it was welded into a homogeneous instrument of war by the discipline, unique for
the times, that Gustavus maintained, and by
the magnetism of his leadership.

Moreover, the numerous foreign elements must
not blind us to the fact that native Swedes
formed nearly 60 per cent of the total, and with
the Scots were the backbone of the army.   Wellington's army at Waterloo was fully as mixed,
but we regard the battle, and rightly, as a
triumph of British staunchness.   The Swedish
raw material was ideal, stout - hearted, inured
to hardship, and with a deep-rooted affection
for the crown, because of the way the Vasa
family had always befriended them against the
nobles.   Again, though their pay was not high,
it was regularly paid during the life of Gustavus—in striking contrast to other armies of
this time who had to rely almost entirely on
plunder.   Instead of the customary haphazard
manner of living on the country, Gustavus
organised a methodical system of requisitions
and fed his troops, as far as possible, from

magazines established at suitable centres, with a regular staff of commissaries who distributed provisions to the regiments in bulk. Not only did this, one of the most notable of his reforms, prevent his forces dispersing over the country-side to forage and pillage, but it avoided the other common danger of waste—the need for repeated moves into fresh districts. Moreover, it enabled him to reduce the swollen baggage-trains and hordes of camp-followers that were a feature of seventeenth century armies, and the worst possible brake on mobility. In one army of 40,000 men, no fewer than 140,000 camp-followers are said to have been counted!

His troops also were systematically quartered, and if occupying a fortified camp were provided with huts or tents; in neither case was dis-cipline relaxed, and the troops were kept up to the mark by properly organised camp and garrison duties. He was also the father of the modern medical service, appointing surgeons to every regiment and allocating a tithe of all booty for the upkeep of the military hospitals.

With troops so well cared for and so well kept in hand, the maintenance of regular discipline was made possible, and was aided by the strong religious feeling which permeated the Swedish Army. Like Cromwell with his " Ironsides " later, Gustavus preferred " such men as made some conscience of what they did," and believed that those who prayed best fought best. Gustavus fully understood the binding and driving force of religion, and even the "New Model" could not excel the Swedish Army in mixing prayer and powder into an explosive compound that would shatter all resistance. Gustavus introduced regular morning and evening prayers, and distributed through the army a special soldiers' Prayer-Book, and the common sight of generals and privates kneeling side by side in prayer left an indelible impression on observers in Germany. But if religion was used as a driving force, it unquestionably proved a civilising influence, and the good behaviour and humanity of the Swedish troops became a matter of wonder to the German people, Protestants and Catholics alike, accustomed to regard a protecting army as only a lesser evil than an invading one. In this connection, a point of note is that in the 'Articles of War,' which he wrote in his own hand and published before his first Polish campaign, among the offences punishable by death were pillage, violence to women, and, rather quaintly, "despising divine service, third offence." This new military code of his is yet another claim to modernism, and has served as a model for subsequent military law. It was administered by two kinds of court, a higher and a lower, corresponding in function and scope to our " general " and " district " courts-martial. The lower was a regimental court with the commanding officer as president, and " assessors " elected by the whole regiment as members. The code was severe—for a regiment which ran away in action the penalty was the old Roman one of decimation, and the regiment had to do the dirty work of the camp until it retrieved itself. Yet in several respects it was more humane than in nineteenth century armies —in the guarantees it provided against injustice and in the absence of flogging. Similarly the Swedish code compares favourably with certain Continental armies of the present generation in its ban on striking private soldiers, and on duelling among officers. The story goes that Gustavus on one occasion yielded to the entreaties of two of his officers and granted special permission for them to meet, and added that he would attend himself. On arrival, he said to the duellists : " Now, gentlemen, at it, and stop you not till one is killed. Moreover, I have the provost-marshal with me, who will at once execute the other "—a pleasant prospect !

While in general the behaviour of the Swedish troops was exemplary, whether in the territory of friends or foes, and in shining contrast to the customs of the age, it is, of course, possible to exaggerate these good qualities. Time and the hero-worshipping historian are apt to throw a halo round the noble figures of the past, to depict them as angels rather than human beings, and when there is real warrant for admiration this tendency is increased. Under the pressure of circumstances, when supplies from Sweden failed we have the King's own testimony, in a letter to Oxenstierna, that "we have been obliged to carry on the war *ex rapto*, with great injury and damage to our neighbours. . . . We have nothing to satisfy the soldiers except what we take by pillage and brigandage." In Gustavus himself, though the *preux chevalier* of his age, a vein of shrewdness underlay his naturally humane disposition. Thus in the Polish campaign we find him writing: "In order to win over as many of the Poles as possible, the field-marshal will not only forbid all pillage . . . in Polish territory, and punish rigorously all excesses of this kind, but he will favour their commerce in every way possible." In contrast, in his address to the troops before Breitenfeld, he is not so much above his time as to omit the time-honoured incitement : "Now you have in front of you, for the first time, a camp filled with precious booty, afterwards a road which passes the sumptuous villages and fertile lands of the Catholics. All that is the price of a single victory."

Happily for his higher fame, acts proved better than words suggested, though acts of plunder were sufficient that year to call from Gustavus a general exhortation to the troops, and a number of executions. But such minor blemishes may well be overlooked in the radiance of his conduct and that of his troops in Bavaria. Here the peasantry maintained a guerilla war of the most atrocious type—even in 1914 the Bavarian troops acquired special notoriety,—hundreds of Swedish soldiers caught singly or in small parties were tortured to death, yet Gustavus refrained from revenge. At Landshut, incensed by a special crop of outrages, he declared to the inhabitants : " You deserve to be annihilated by fire and sword," but on a voice from the crowd asking if the King of Sweden, admired for his clemency, was now to enter upon the bloody path of vengeance, Gustavus changed his intention, and maintained his moderation to the end.

III.

Turning now to his more material reforms, his influence on arms and equipment calls for notice. He stands out in history as the first commander to grasp the importance of fire, and, in particular, that infantry fire-power was the route of progress and the key to the future. He introduced the wheel-lock and the cartridge, lightened and shortened the musket so as to do away with the fork or rest which had formerly been necessary, reduced the number of loading motions—all aids to mobility and hitting power. Hitherto the musketeers had been regarded as little better than auxiliaries to the true infantry, the pikemen, and their numbers had only been half those of the pikemen. With improved firearms Gustavus increased the proportion of musketeers to two-thirds of a force—until the bayonet was invented musketeers were defenceless while reloading (a process of some ninety-nine motions !), and so pikemen were still necessary, though now more as a protective than as an offensive arm. More notable still, Gustavus often used his musketeers on independent missions, and later formed entire regiments of them, employing them to accompany his cavalry on some swift blow at an enemy detachment or garrison— an innovation that well entitles him to be considered the father of infantry mobility. In this connection, it is interesting to find that in his Polish wars he revived the device of the English archers at Creçy and the Hundred Years' War—the musketeers, when unguarded by pikemen, carrying sharpened palisades in order to erect an emergency protection if charged by cavalry, from behind which they could fire. After a time, however, these were carried in the train, as Gustavus realised that, next to fire, mobility was the supreme asset of infantry.

From the weapons of the Swedish infantry, we pass to their tactics, where again Gustavus laid the foundations on which subsequent ages built. Hitherto the infantry had been formed in huge and unwieldy squares, as many as fifty ranks deep, under the mistaken impression that density meant strength, that the more men one crowded together implied increased power of resistance and impulsion of attack. The fact shows how backward were the seventeenth century methods compared with those of the ancient world, and how little study and intelligent reflection had been devoted to the lessons of Roman history. Nearly two thousand years after the Macedonian phalanx had gone down before the flexible and articulated legion of the Romans, which with its distances between lines and intervals between units allowed troops room to manœuvre and use their weapons, we find the armies of Europe repeating the futilities of the phalanx—and with the greater error because artillery was now in existence to shatter its cumbrous mass.   These " battles " or " tertia " of the Spanish style remained in use by all armies save that of the Swedes ; with the pikemen inside, and the musketeers gathered in smaller squares at the four corners— resembling the turrets of a castle in plan— clearing away to the flanks when the forces came to grips.

Gustavus broke up these unwieldy formations and arranged his men only six deep with intervals between the files, while the musketeers commonly closed into three deep for firing. This three-deep formation became the pattern for all subsequent tactical evolution, the precursor of the modern firing-line.   The measure of Gustavus's reform may be gauged by the fact that nearly two centuries passed before a further reduction to a two-deep line took place ; not until 1824 was the latter adopted in the British drill-book, though it had been habitually used under Wellington in the Peninsula.   If we reflect on war in the light of its three basic elements—power to hit, power to

move, and power to guard,—we can appreciate
the wisdom and benefits of the change. For
by these more extended and thinner formations
the volume of fire was increased, manœuvre
made possible, and the effects of enemy fire
diminished.

It is little wonder that, generalship apart,
the Austro-Spanish phalanxes went down before
the modern legions of Gustavus, even as their
forebears at Cynoscephalæ in 197 B.C.

But there was more in the Swedish formations
than simply a reduction of the ranks, and this
additional factor is an historical point which,
so far as the writer can trace, has been undis-
covered hitherto, or at any rate its importance
and significance overlooked. This point springs
from the peculiar cross-shaped formation often
adopted by the Swedish *brigade*—which was
the new tactical unit of Gustavus's army, and
the strength of which was a variable quantity,
between 1000 and 2000 men. It was a period
of transition, and as a natural consequence
formations as well as establishments were still
in a state of fluidity, subject to frequent change
and experiment, and the fact that other
formations were also in use has tended to cloak
the purpose and value of this one which was
used at Brietenfeld, and is handed down to us
in Lord Reay's sketch. Another probable cause

of the oversight was that with the disappearance
of pikemen the infantry formations of Europe
took the linear form that characterised them
down to 1918, when the method of deploying
infantry into waves or lines, only able to attack
direct to their front, was at last superseded
by that of little combat groups, distributed in
considerable depth, which were able to infiltrate
between, and attack in front and flank simultaneously, the posts of the enemy.   Accustomed
to linear formations, it was but natural that
military historians should fail to perceive the
design and advantage of the Swedish " cross," or
rather inverted T.   Still a further cause lies per-
chance in the fact that the sketches bequeathed
to us by Lord Reay and others show only a
single brigade, or demi-brigade ; it is only by
plotting a line of such brigades that the true
inwardness of their formation becomes apparent.   This formation may best be explained
by a diagram, and as can at once be seen,
the advanced centre division of pikemen formed

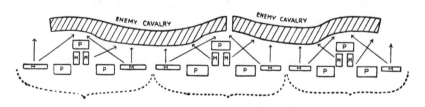

P = PIKEMEN   M = MUSKETEERS

a " spearhead " in attack or a breakwater in
defence, calculated to disorganise the enemy's
array while the divisions of musketeers, thus
" refused " and protected from the initial shock,
and with their flanks protected also by other
divisions of pikemen, were able to assail the
enemy with fire from front and flank respec-
tively and, incidentally, to protect the flanks
and sweep the front of their own forward division
of pikemen.   Not only was such a formation
ideal for the conditions of the time, but it was
markedly ahead in tactical conception of those
that prevailed during subsequent centuries, for
it fulfilled in the realm of fire-tactics the grand
tactical formula of a convergent blow from two
directions, striking the enemy in front and
flank simultaneously.   In the higher scale of
tactics this has ever been the master-key to
victory of the Great Captains, but not until
the closing stages of the war of 1914-18 was
it translated into the lower scale of the infantry
units.   Thus the discovery that its germ at
least is to be found in the wars of Gustavus,
is a supreme tribute to his transcendent grasp
of military science, and one more link in his
claim to be the founder of modern war.

Passing from infantry to cavalry we find the
same vision of the true principles.   In other
armies they, too, were formed in masses, some-

times ten deep. Worse still, they had become
so enamoured of their new firearms as to forget
that in the impulsion of the charge has ever
lain the special strength of cavalry action.
Infantry can disorganise an enemy force, can
destroy it piecemeal, but only cavalry, because
of the momentum of the onslaught, can *shatter*
it and break up its organisation irretrievably—
in other words, cavalry is essentially the decisive
arm.   It is because the deadliness and range
of present-day firearms have rendered the cavalry
charge impossible and made tactics lop-sided,
that recent warfare has grown so indecisive,
producing the stagnation of 1914-18 and the
helplessness of generalship to recreate a war of
movement.   Fortunately science has come to
our rescue and provided us with an armoured
and mechanical charger—the tank ; when it is
realised that the latter is but the modern form
of cavalry, and should be employed as such, in
the swift tank assault of to-morrow we shall
see the rebirth of the cavalry charge—and with
it the decisive warfare of the Great Captains.
When Gustavus appeared on the scene, cavalry
had lost sight of its proper rôle, and was accustomed to trot up to the enemy's line, when
each rank would discharge their pieces, and
then wheel off to reload.

Gustavus revived the cavalry charge and

reduced the ranks to four, and later three; the front rank only were to fire their pistols, and then the whole line to charge with drawn swords at the gallop. It is a testimony to his mingled vision and balance—he was no one-sided fanatic—that in the same measure as he developed the fire action of infantry, he restored the shock action of cavalry.

It is a common statement that Gustavus mixed infantry with his horsemen, which if true would seem a serious mistake, but closer study makes it clear that these were but small detachments of 180 musketeers placed in the intervals between the regiments of cavalry, when drawn up in order of battle; and that he did this in order to give them greater defensive power and help to break up the enemy's initial onset, as his own cavalry were inferior in numbers and not so well mounted.

Furthermore, while retaining the heavy siege-guns in common use he introduced a new type of light regimental piece, which one horse or three men could move. It was an iron four-pounder, and the charge in a thin round wooden case was wired to the ball—the first artillery cartridge. Lighter, more handy, with its cartridge always ready, this *pièce Suedoise* could be fired faster than the musket and, adopted afterwards in other armies, was the prototype of

the field-gun.   To this invention and its employment—the manœuvring power and rapidity
of fire of his batteries—Gustavus owed no small
share of his tactical success.

Hitherto the artillery had consisted only of
heavy pieces, requiring as many as thirty-six
horses to draw the heaviest, and sixteen horses
even to draw the culverin, which fired an 18-
pound shot.   As the teams were hired and the
gunners even were often civilians, once posted
they could rarely be moved, and in case of defeat
were inevitably lost.   Gustavus experimented
with the so-called leather cannon, consisting of
a thin copper tube strengthened by iron bands
and covered with leather, but after the Polish
wars abandoned it in favour of his new short
4-pounder cast-iron gun, which was more effective
and reliable while nearly as handy.   Grape and
canister were generally fired from these field-
guns, round shot only from the siege-guns.

We may also note that Gustavus organised
a corps of engineers, and though his permanent
fortifications hold little new, he notably developed the methods of field-fortification.   He
drilled the whole army in throwing these up,
and in pontoon-bridging, while making full use
of expert aid and even of civilian scientists.
In one respect his temporary defences are a
striking forecast of present practice, for instead

of a single line of continuous works, he would build a series of mutually supporting but separate posts distributed in depth in two or more lines.

Gustavus is sometimes called the inventor of uniform, and though this is not strictly true, he did much to develop uniformity in dress and, even more, utility for the conditions of his campaigns. Early in his reign the troops served in their peasant's dress, apart from the uniformed royal bodyguard, but by establishing clothing depots he gradually ensured that all wore clothing of a uniform pattern— a sleeveless tunic and loose breeches, their legs clad in coarse woollen stockings, and their feet in shoes or bootees, according to the season. By improving the warmth and weatherproofness of the clothing, Gustavus was enabled to conduct his winter campaigns—a rarity then.

Thus, to summarise, his supreme achievement was to create the first scientifically designed instrument of war of modern times, blending hitting power, guarding power, and mobility ; in which the fire of infantry was first developed as a main factor in battle and their formations made flexible, the true shock rôle of cavalry was revived—so giving scope to their distinctive qualities of mobility and moral effect, and the new factor, artillery, established as a third arm of the service. By teaching them the lesson of mutual support towards a common objective, he founded combined tactics. Finally, by putting his forces on a permanent basis and binding them together through a regular discipline, he produced the first real war-machine which, with its parts properly fitted, oiled by co-operation, and tuned by experience, developed a power and speed of action against which the cumbrous and rigid armies of the time could not compete. In each of the several elements—hitting power, guarding power, and mobility—the Swedish Army excelled the Imperial forces, and in combining the three it broke away altogether from the past and ushered in a new era of warfare.

As to the manner in which this instrument was employed—the sphere of strategy and grand tactics—and how far Gustavus was a pioneer in what Marshal Saxe termed "the sublime branches of the art of war," a brief survey of his German campaigns may best show.

IV.

The operations of Gustavus during his first year in Germany, though their narration and discussion might well fill a volume, were not of a decisive character, nor did they exercise a far-reaching effect on the struggle, save in so far as they paved the way for the greater moves to follow. From his landing, on 4th July 1630 until September 1631, when the Elector of Saxony, driven at last to abandon his neutrality in face of the Imperial ultimatum and invasion of his dominions, concluded an alliance with Gustavus, the latter's efforts were directed to secure and expand his base of operations on the Baltic coast. This limited action was forced on him not only by the need to secure his communications with Sweden and build up his strength, but even more by the failure of the German Protestant states to rally to the support of the man who had come to save them. Even the Duke of Pomerania, the province where he landed and one that had suffered grievously from the exactions of the Imperial troops, had to be forced into alliance by the appearance of the Swedish army at the gates of Stettin, his capital. As for the two chief Protestant princes, the Electors of Saxony and Brandenburg, they held aloof until late in the summer of 1631.

If Gustavus appears over-cautious during this first stage, this lack of support and the smallness of his own forces are ample justification, while, apart from its limited scope, his strategy has *method* behind it—a feature new to the warfare of the age, and perhaps better conceived in this phase than in his own subsequent campaigns.

The hallmark of real strategy is that it deter-
mines what is the object and maintains it unswervingly, *adjusting both the means to the end
and the end to the means.*

By the end of 1630, Gustavus was master
of almost the whole of Pomerania, and had
penetrated into Mecklenburg. He finished that
year on a note of triumph by the storm of
Greifenhagen and Garz, when by all the orthodox
customs he should have been resting in winter
quarters. Like other stereotyped soldiers confronted with novel means and methods of war,
the Imperial commanders must have felt that
Gustavus "was not playing the game." The
Romans called Hannibal perfidious because he
practised the principle of surprise ; the Chevalier
Bayard, "*sans peur et sans reproche*," invariably
put to death musketeers and other users of gunpowder, and recent instances of the same attitude need no reference.

In February 1631, while Tilly was collecting
the Imperial forces for an advance against
Gustavus, the Elector of Saxony called a meeting
of the Protestant princes at Leipsig, to which
Gustavus's envoy was not even admitted. The
conclave bore no fruit, as the assemblage, instead
of raising armies, devoted their time and erudi-
tion to the futile task of drawing up respectful
memorials to the Emperor, setting forth their

grievances, which could only be redressed, as they had been inflicted, with sword in hand.

Meanwhile Tilly was preparing to besiege the famous city and Protestant stronghold of Magdeburg, after an abortive move towards Gustavus, on the Oder, and a spell of manœuvring on both sides. Hindered by the neutral attitude of Brandenburg and Saxony from a direct move to succour the threatened city, which lay so far from his base, Gustavus attempted by exploits on the Oder to draw Tilly again thither. This move failing, he set out in May on its direct relief. But on arrival at Berlin, time was wasted in negotiations with the vacillating Elector of Brandenburg for the possession of Custrin and Spandau—it was risky to advance farther with two such fortresses in his rear held by a doubtful neutral. Only by the threat of force did he secure them, and then the next hitch occurred : the Elector of Saxony, afraid of the Emperor, objected to the passage of the Swedish Army through his territory. As the strongest Protestant prince, Gustavus could not afford to antagonise one whom he wanted as an ally, and ere negotiations were completed Magdeburg had fallen —the horrors of its sack are engraved deeply in history. Falling back on Pomerania for a while, in July Gustavus again advanced, up the Elbe towards Tilly. After more manœuvring came

the decisive act which forced John George of
Saxony, having sat so long on the fence, to
jump down on the Swedish side. Disregarding
his protests and entreaties, the Emperor through
Tilly ordered the Elector to join forces against
the Swedes, and while he hesitated, the Imperial
army invaded and began ravaging his lands.
A desperate appeal to Gustavus for aid was
followed by the treaty of alliance that the
Swedish King had so long desired, and while
Tilly occupied Leipsig, the combined armies
moved to meet him.

Tilly had taken up a strong position in front
of Leipsig and was awaiting reinforcements,
but the urgings of the impetuous Pappenheim,
eager for battle, led him to go forward and
offer battle instead of awaiting it. The plain
north of the city, stretching for miles and marked
only by slight undulations, formed an ideal
arena for an old-style battle, placing no check
on the free movement of the forces, if its very
absence of obstacles debarred the subtle ruses of
generalship—little matter in an age when the
principle of surprise was rarely exploited and its
value largely unrealised. Here, betwixt but in
advance of the villages of Seehausen and Breitenfeld, on the crest of a gentle slope, Tilly drew
up his army in order of battle, covering a front
of about two and a half miles. Controversy has

raged on many of the details, not least Tilly's
original dispositions, but the main phases are
clear. Historians differ as to whether Tilly drew
up his army in one line or in two, as was the
usual custom, but it would seem most probable
that it was originally formed in two, with a
reserve in the rear, rather to the right centre
behind the guns and on a slight elevation. When,
however, the rout of the Saxons gave him the
opportunity to move his infantry to the right
to attack the exposed flank of the Swedes, he
pushed the " battalia " of his second line forward into the intervals of the first line for the
purpose of this oblique move and attack. The infantry formed thirteen or seventeen solid squares,
of from 1500 to 2000 men apiece. Tilly's cavalry
were on the two wings, as was customary, Pappenheim on the left, Furstenburg and Isolani on
the right, a total of about 10,000 cavalry, making
altogether an army of about 35,000—rather less
than the combined forces of the Swedes and
Saxons, but, after the early rout of the latter,
far superior to the Swedes alone. Only in guns
had Tilly a marked inferiority, not more than
thirty-six to fully a hundred against him. In
appearance his splendid-looking array of veterans
contrasted strikingly with the tattered and war-
soiled troops of the Swedes or the immaculately
equipped but untried Saxons.

Early in the morning of 7th September 1631 the allied armies, in two columns, Swedes on the right and Saxons on the left, crossed the Loberbach, a marshy stream running across their front. The formality of the time is well shown by the failure to fall on Gustavus during this crossing. Only Pappenheim with some 2000 cavalry went forward to hinder the advance, but the Scots of the vanguard, supported by some dragoons, drove him back. Thereafter unhindered, save by the smoke from the burning village of Podelwitz—set on fire by Pappenheim in falling back,—Gustavus formed his army in two lines and a reserve. On his left was drawn up the Saxon Army.

By noon the armies were in position, and the battle opened with an artillery duel, in which Torstenson's guns fired three shots to the Imperialists' one. This continued for over two hours, when at last the real action began. The fiery Pappenheim, without awaiting orders, moved his cavalry to the left to outflank the Swedish right, and then swinging round struck at the Swedish flank. The manœuvring power and flexible formation of the Swedes enabled Gustavus to wheel up his second line cavalry at right angles to the first and so form a defensive flank, which, strengthened by musketeers, proved a rampart on which

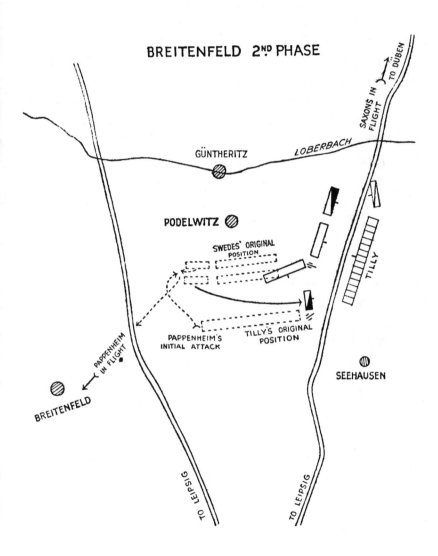

BREITENFELD 2ᴺᴰ PHASE

Pappenheim's cuirassiers broke themselves to pieces.

After seven vain assaults the Imperial cavalry fell back discouraged, and, followed up sharply by the Swedes, were driven in flight from the field. Meanwhile critical events had been taking place on the other wing. The Imperial cavalry, under Furstenburg, had fallen on the Saxons, and in a short half hour almost the whole army, infantry and cavalry alike, were in disorderly flight—thus laying bare the flank of the Swedes.

Up to now Tilly had neither ordered nor controlled the action, which seemed likely to degenerate into a "soldiers' battle," but the rout of the Saxons and a flash of inspiration, of true generalship, gave him the chance to regain the reins of command, and in doing so attempt what well might have been a decisive coup. He ordered his centre to move to the right and follow in the wake of Furstenburg, and by an oblique march brought his heavy infantry "battles" into line on the flank of the Swedes. It was a manœuvre in which we can perhaps find the germ of Frederick the Great's famous "oblique order" of attack. But he was meeting an alert, not a supine enemy, and one, moreover, whose flexible formations enabled him to manœuvre more quickly than Tilly's unwieldy squares.

Horn, commanding the Swedish cavalry on this wing, swung back his first line and wheeled up his second to oppose a new front to this attack in flank, while Gustavus hurried infantry from his second line to reinforce him and prolong the line. Fortunately, also, the cumbrous formations of the Imperialists, disarrayed by their flank move, were a handicap to rapid action, and their attack became a disjointed instead of a concentrated blow.

While the scales of victory hang in the balance, there comes the decisive stroke ; with his right wing now secure since Pappenheim's flight, Gustavus himself, taking a large part of his right wing cavalry, sweeps round and over Tilly's original position, where his guns are still, cutting him off from Leipsig. The captured guns are turned to enfilade Tilly's present left flank, while Torstenson with the Swedish artillery pounds his front, and Gustavus makes a general wheel with his centre and right to attack the Imperial left. Assailed in front and partly in flank, with their close-packed ranks torn by a double weight of artillery fire, the rigid and immobile Imperial squares can but offer a hopeless resistance. The end is inevitable, and though their stand is magnificent, nightfall finds the scattered remnants in headlong flight. It was a victory of dramatic decisiveness—that evening the long invincible Imperial army, under the iron heel of which all Germany had lain prone in ruin or terror, was scattered to the winds, not merely defeated but destroyed for all practical purposes of resistance. Apart from an actual loss of about 12,000, the fugitives were so dispersed that Tilly on his retreat could rally but 600, and Pappenheim only another 1400.

What were the factors that brought victory ? Not any epoch-making novelty in conception or in manœuvre, for so far as we can tell Gustavus planned a battle of the typical parallel order, and such attacks in flanks as developed were the outcome of the Imperialists' change of position rather than of deliberate out-flanking manœuvres. The rebirth of grand tactics was still in the future ; indeed there was perhaps more approach to it in Pappenheim's attack, or Tilly's exploitation of the Saxon rout for his oblique move.

So far as Gustavus's generalship counted in the victory, it was by his quickness in rein-forcing threatened points in face of an able opponent and, above all, his true *coup d'œil* in seizing the moment for a decisive counter-move, and the vigour with which he pressed it home. He proved himself as fine a battle-captain as any in the roll of history. But the

main cause of the victory lay in the instrument
he had forged, and the story of the battle makes
clear how the superior fire and manœuvring
power of its component parts proved decisive
in each phase, whether in defence or attack.

The victory struck terror into the hearts of
the Empire—Vienna was said to be "dumb
with fright," Bohemian forests were laid low
to block the road, the walls of cities hundreds
of miles from the battlefield were kept manned.

Whither would Gustavus move, and how
would he exploit his great victory?

For the moment the Emperor could raise no
effective forces to oppose his advance. At a
council of war the Elector of Saxony, Count
Horn, and many other officers advocated an
immediate advance on the Imperial capital.
More notable still, Oxenstierna the prudent,
though not present at Breitenfeld, was strongly
in favour of this plan. But Gustavus decided
otherwise—to move into South-West Germany,
giving as his reasons that he did not wish to
lose sight of Tilly, and that he wished to make
use of the resources of the Catholic dioceses
there for the maintenance of his army, so allowing the Protestants of North Germany a chance
to recuperate.

Whether his decision was guided by the
highest wisdom is a moot point. Those who

support it point to the value of consolidating
his position, of rallying new friends to his
standard, and simultaneously gaining a grip
on the territories of the Catholic League—
thus he could organise a fresh centre of
Protestant power before attempting greater
schemes.

On the other hand, we need to remember
that this move on the Rhine earned him the
distrust of France, his ally, and that never
again did the Imperial power appear so shaken,
or its seat so defenceless, as on the morrow of
Breitenfeld. Was a supreme strategical opportunity lost ?

When Oxenstierna met Gustavus shortly
afterwards, he saluted the King thus : " I
would felicitate you at Vienna on the victory
you have just gained," and eighteen years
after the death of the King, said of him : " If,
after the battle of Leipsig, he had penetrated
into the hereditary States of the Empire, instead
of marching on the Rhine, and had left the
States of Germany to arrange among themselves, the Emperor would have found it impossible to continue the war."

Following his decision, Gustavus advanced
into Franconia and down the Main, clearing
its fortresses ; then across the Rhine at Mainz,
pushing down as far as Mannheim. After this

he went into winter quarters, establishing his
court at Frankfort-on-the-Main. What a change
from the previous winter! Then his troops
eked out a bare existence on the scanty resources of desolate Pomerania, whereas now
they lived in unwonted luxury on the rich lands
of Franconia. Then neither prince nor city
dared avow their alliance with the man who
had risked all to come to their aid; now Gustavus's court was a brilliant spectacle, where
the ambassadors from every European country
came to pay their respects to the victorious
monarch, the most flattered and courted
sovereign in Europe, whose very name struck
awe and fear into Catholic hearts. Yet everything hinged on Gustavus's life, and threats
and rumours of assassination were frequent,
though his very contempt of precautions was
in some ways a safeguard. Urged to keep a
bodyguard about him, he is said to have replied:
"Then you would have me disregard the protection of God?" A significant light on his
own feeling and sense of duty is thrown by
another utterance: "Believe me, I love a
comfortable life as well as any man, and I have
no desire to die an early death. The Emperor
would readily make a separate peace with me
to get me to return to Sweden. But I dare
not leave so many innocent people subject to

his revenge. Were it not for this, I would soon
get me gone."

The campaign reopened next spring, when
Tilly, who had been operating on the higher
reaches of the Main and had defeated Horn at
Bamberg, retired in face of Gustavus's approach,
falling back on the Danube to cover Bavaria.
Following him up, Gustavus passed through
Nuremburg and on to Donauwörth, where he
secured the crossing of the Danube. Just east
of this town the little river Lech flows into the
Danube from the south, and forms with the
Danube a rampart for Bavaria. The Danube
forms the southern boundary of a rough square
of which the Rhine forms the west side, the
Main the north, and a line from Bamberg to
the Danube at Donauwörth marks the east side.
Thus Gustavus had moved along the north side
and down the east, which was prolonged by the
Lech. On the Lech just above its junction with
the Danube lies Rain, which Tilly had occupied,
breaking down the bridge near the town, and
no other existed nearer than Augsburg, twenty
miles up-stream.

At a spot where the swift-flowing river made
a bend to the west, forming a salient towards
the Swedes, Gustavus established seventy-two
guns to command the passage. Meanwhile, by
a personal reconnaissance, he discovered another

possible passage a mile up-stream, where there was a small island in mid-river. At both points he began bridges, the first under cover of a heavy fire, the second unknown to the enemy, though he moved eighteen guns thither to cover the passage. At the first point, by setting fire to wet straw, he created a smoke screen to cloak the crossing—a method of concealment foreshadowing World War developments, when, improved by science, it became a vital factor. Did not Ludendorff declare that tanks and smoke were the two most dangerous enemies the German armies had to face in the final phases of the war ?

Meanwhile at the surprise point 300 Finns, picked men under Colonel Wrangel, were sent over in boats, brought from the Danube in carts, to secure a covering position on the far bank. Though discovered and attacked, they held on until the bridge was completed as far as the island, when Gustavus crossed with two brigades of infantry, wading the last part covered by the fire of the guns on the other bank.

By this double forcing of the passage Tilly was assailed from two directions simultaneously, unable to defend either adequately, and in the fierce fight which ensued his forces were driven back, and he was mortally wounded. Under cover of night the Bavarians, now taken charge of by the Elector Maximilian, retreated to the east, to Ingolstadt on the Danube, thus laying bare to Gustavus the path into Bavaria.

The passage of the Lech is a model for subsequent generations, perhaps indeed Gustavus's tactical masterpiece, in the double crossing and convergent attack from two directions, in the way it forecast the possibilities of mobile artillery and their concentration, and not least in the King's boldness in face of a deep and torrential river with a strongly posted enemy behind it. To-day, when the advent of tanks has endowed river barriers and the problems of forcing them with special importance, this feat repays study, not least in the use of a primitive smoke screen.

But in one vital point—exploitation of success, by which alone the fruits of victory can be garnered—he was still enchained by the habits of his age. Small blame really, for not until Napoleon was the value of pursuit developed.

Thus after this success he made no attempt to pursue, nor even to follow up and destroy the forces of Maximilian before passing on into Bavaria—an omission that was to cost him dear.

From the Lech onwards his progress was a triumphant and unopposed march, Augsburg, Munich—the Bavarian capital,—and all the places south of the Danube opening their gates to him without resistance. His conquering advance

had brought him from the shores of the Baltic
to the foot of the Alps. At the same time the
Elector of Saxony, who had undertaken the direct
advance towards Vienna through Bohemia, entered
Prague without firing a shot.

But at the very moment when the arms of
Protestantism shone in the full blaze of noon-
tide glory, a cloud loomed on the horizon. With
Tilly dead, there was but one man, capable
of the task, to whom the Emperor could turn
in his extremity. To the envoys of Ferdinand
the dismissed Wallenstein at first declined to
listen, allowing their entreaties to grow ever
more desperate, to pave the way for the ultimate
disclosure of his terms—terms so humiliating
as no subject before or since has dared to ask
of his sovereign. So critical was the position
that the Emperor granted them almost abjectly,
and within a couple of months, as if by the wave
of a magician's wand, a fresh and splendidly
equipped army of 40,000 veterans had rallied
to Wallenstein's banner. With this, the same
week that Gustavus entered Munich, Wallenstein chased the Saxons out of Prague and
then back over the borders of Bohemia—
while Maximilian of Bavaria moved to join
him. Far-sighted and a master of politico-
military strategy, Wallenstein used his pleni-
potentiary authority to offer the Elector of

Saxony a separate peace on most favourable terms.

Alarmed for his communications with the Baltic, endangered not only by Wallenstein's northward move but by the possible defection of the Saxons, Gustavus, outwitted in the first move of the new game, was forced to quit Bavaria in an attempt to prevent the junction of Wallenstein and Maximilian.   Too late to do this, and as he was only able to concentrate some 18,000 troops for the purpose—a strategical lapse considering the 100,000 he had in Germany,—too weak to risk an attack on the combined armies, he fell back on Nuremburg, partly because it was a central point between the Rhine country, Franconia, and Bavaria, but more because he did not like to abandon his faithful adherents to the Imperial vengeance. Strategically a move to the Main would seem wiser, as here he would be better placed for reinforcements, and in touch with Saxony.

At Nuremburg he built a vast entrenched camp and awaited reinforcements.   Wallenstein leisurely followed him but would not risk an attack, despite Maximilian's urgings, until he had trained his army and all conditions were in his favour.   Instead, knowing that time was on his side, as he commanded Gustavus's communications, he entrenched a camp opposite the city, about four miles away, in order to starve out Gustavus. A prolonged "famine" match ensued, with many combats between foraging parties, in which the superiority of Wallenstein's light horse, especially the Croats under Isolani, gave him the advantage.

In vain Gustavus offered battle when his reinforcements arrived—only to complicate the food problem—until at last in desperation he decided to assault Wallenstein's fortified position. He concentrated his attack against the hill crowned by an old fortress, the Alte Feste, which was both the key of the position and its strongest point. After a desperate struggle—the hottest fighting of the entire campaign—the Swedes were repulsed. For two weeks more the starving armies remained face to face, and then on the 18th September—two and a half months from the start—Gustavus marched away, after one last formal challenge to battle. Three days later Wallenstein broke up his camp and followed. It had been a contest of will-power, with famine the chief weapon, and Wallenstein had won. From a military point of view it appears a poor success and a poorer method, but Wallenstein was playing for political rather than military stakes. In the eyes of Europe Gustavus had received his first check.

The next round of the contest opened. Gustavus with his main force moved south on the
Danube, still bent on his methodical plan of
consolidating a strong Protestant Union, the
Corpus Evangelicorum, and extending its area
in Southern Germany. Partly also he may
have hoped by threatening Bavaria and the
southern approach to Austria to draw Wallenstein away from Saxony and the King's communications with the Baltic. But for this
game of manœuvring against each other's rear,
Wallenstein was the better placed, as his base
was Bohemia and he occupied a central position
from which he could operate on interior lines
against the Protestant forces.

Moreover, his strategical insight appears the
truer, for instead of following the bait he moved
north-east into Saxony in pursuance of his
aim of detaching the Elector from the Swedish
alliance. Both sides were violating the modern
doctrine of seeking out the main forces of the
enemy, but whereas Gustavus left his rival
across his communications, Wallenstein knew,
and was striking at, the Achilles' heel of the
Swedish power. Only a military pedant would
deny his wisdom. Unswervingly he fulfilled
the principle of direction in his strategy,
and Gustavus, receiving news of Wallenstein's
invasion of Saxony and the Elector's appeals

for aid, was forced to conform. Abandoning
his designs in the Danube country he hurried
northward, and by a series of rapid marches—
Donauwörth to Naumburg, some 200 miles in
eighteen days,—caught up with his adversary.
If Wallenstein better fulfilled the principle
of direction, Gustavus far excelled him in
those of mobility and concentration. The Imperial general made no attempt to beat the
Protestant forces in detail, and only sought
passively to keep the Saxons and Swedes
separated.

Gustavus paused at Naumburg, sixty miles
from his rival at Leipsig, to concentrate his
forces for battle and await reinforcements. As
he had thrown up entrenchments Wallenstein
thought he did not mean to attack, and so
allowed Pappenheim to lay siege to Moritzburg,
near Halle, himself moving to Lützen, south-
west of Leipsig. But immediately Gustavus
heard of Pappenheim's departure he determined
to strike, even though still inferior in numbers—
trusting in the superiority of his instrument.
This instant seizure of the chance afforded by
the enemy's dispersion is an admirable example
of decisiveness and energy in fulfilling the
principle of concentration *du fort au faible*.
His approach was, however, signalled to Wallenstein, who sent Pappenheim an urgent message

to return, and despatched Isolani's Croats to
delay the Swedish advance. Though the Croats
were soon driven back, they had gained for
Wallenstein a respite that had an important
bearing on the battle. For had Gustavus been
able to attack that day, the 6th of November,
Pappenheim could have taken no share in the
battle. The Imperial army, curiously, was drawn
up parallel with the Leipsig road and the Swedish
line of advance, instead of across it ; with its
right, however, protected by the village of Lützen.

As the Swedes were marching directly on
Wallenstein's flank, an attack on this would
seem the obvious course, but instead Gustavus
diverged to the right to avoid Lützen, and
drew up in battle order parallel to the Imperial
army. Though one shrewdly suspects that the
sacrifice of such an obvious opportunity was
due to the custom of the time, it is fair to point
out several better reasons for his action.

Such an attack, if successful, would drive
Wallenstein back on Leipsig, whereas Gustavus's
object was to push him away from the Elector's
territory, and at the same time himself unite
with the Saxons. Secondly, if Pappenheim
returned he would automatically take the
Swedes in flank. Thirdly, to attack through
a village might well throw the troops into disorder—as with Frederick's Prussians at Kolin

a century later. The last objection, however, does not meet the argument that he might have attacked the Imperial army obliquely in rear, while sending a detachment of cavalry to hold off Pappenheim's possible return, a manœuvre against which the immobile Imperial masses would have been helpless. But such a conception was beyond the seventeenth century mind, and despite all his " modernism " we must judge Gustavus by the standard of his time, assess him by how much he advanced the art of war, not by how much more he might have advanced it. Furthermore, let us remember that he was cut off at the age of thirty-seven. How great was the scope for further progress had he lived.

It is no purpose of ours to examine in detail the tactics of Lützen beyond its opening, for our concern is with the career of Gustavus, and the decisive acts of the battle took place after his death, when others were in command.

The Swedish formation was similar to that of Breitenfeld, in two lines and a reserve, with the cavalry on the wings. Some have suggested that it was formed obliquely to the German Army, and trace in this the germ of Frederician tactics, but from such facts as we have, the obliqueness appears the result of accident rather than design.

The typical mists of a November morning shrouded the battlefield and obscured the rival hosts. Fate seemed against Gustavus, to whom time was all-important, for not until eleven o'clock did the fog lift and allow the artillery to open fire. It was nearly noon before the King, drawing his sword, gave the word to advance. Across the Imperial front lay the Leipsig road, with its ditches held by musketeers. On the right Gustavus overthrew the Imperial cavalry, but his centre, after getting across the road, was counter-attacked by Wallenstein and driven back, while the left was checked by the fire of the Imperial batteries. Hearing of the recoil of his infantry in the centre, Gustavus hastened thither to lead them back to the attack, and, owing to his impetuosity, perhaps also to his short sight and the fog, he pressed too far ahead of his troops, was wounded by a musket-ball, and then as, faint with loss of blood, he was being helped away, ran into a party of Imperial cuirassiers, at whose hands he met his death. Accounts of his end are conflicting— the fog of nature combined with the fog of battle to shroud this final scene in an isolated corner of the battlefield.

"The pitcher had been carried once too often to the well."

The news of the King's fall infused such

fury into the Swedes that, despite the arrival
of Pappenheim, victory rested on their side
after a grim struggle lasting until evening, when
under cover of darkness the shattered forces of
Wallenstein made good their retreat.

But, robbed of their leader, the Swedes failed
to take advantage of the victory, and the " Thirty
Years' War " that had opened in 1618 was
doomed to drag out another sixteen years, with
France supplanting the Swedes as the leaders
of the combination against the Empire.

In taking leave of this " first of the moderns "
in the realm of warfare, let us pause for a moment
to embody in final shape the various features
brought out by our analysis of his work and
campaigns. As a strategist his supreme contribution to the modern art of war was to intro-
duce *method*, in particular to revive the principle
of security, but his grasp of the principle of
direction—in object and objective—was less full,
coloured unduly by immediate political con-
siderations and his cherished project of the
Corpus Evangelicorum. To be fair, we must
admit that, unlike other Great Captains, he
came on the scene not as a conqueror but as a
liberator, to release a multitude of petty States
from their mental as well as their physical
chains, and to build up a fabric of self-reliant

and mutually supporting units for the lasting preservation of the Reformed Faith. Yet, looking back, it is easy to appreciate that this scheme was impracticable until the power of the Empire and its Catholic satellites was crushed, its will to dictate broken. But if his strategic conception was faulty, his execution in the attainment of his immediate goal marked a great advance in the art of war.

He was the first commander in modern times to fulfil and blend the three elemental principles of war—security, mobility, and concentration, the *tria juncta in uno* which constitute the economic application of force to attain the goal—speedy and profitable victory. That he might have done so more fully is beyond question, but his execution marked a measure of progress such as few of his successors have recorded. Where he falls short is in the higher "direction" of these principles — the use of surprise, concentration against a weak joint in his opponent's armour, exploitation of initial success, whereby the truest economy of force is attained—the maximum result for the minimum cost. To grand tactics, Gustavus contributes no novel manœuvre; he does not attempt to strike the enemy in flank nor to complete his victory by vigorous pursuit; though he has a reserve, it appears to have no tactical function.

His outstanding achievement is in fact the tactical instrument he forged, and the tactical " mechanism " through which this worked its triumphs. He organised the first regular and national army, the first supply service, and laid the foundation of military law and a regular system of discipline. The creator of field artillery and of combined tactics, he developed the modern rôle of infantry and restored the true rôle of cavalry. The pioneer of open and flexible formations, he pointed for subsequent generations the way to counteract the effect of the firearm—that epoch-making invention which uprooted the old foundations of military science. He has been called the author of linear tactics wrongly, for his achievement was far greater— his system was the forerunner not of eighteenth century, but of twentieth century fire-tactics.

In face of such far-reaching and revolutionary reforms and innovations, who can gainsay his right to be entitled " The Founder of Modern War " ?

As a man he ranks even higher, if possible, for his motives were perhaps the noblest and purest that inspired any of the Great Captains, his pursuit of them so unimpassioned and humane as to shine like a solitary beacon amid the dark deeds and hideous ravages of the Thirty Years' War, that left Germany a desert.

He might well be given the further title of " Father of Civilised Warfare," was there not a risk that his spirit, viewing from the eternal shades the deeds of recent generations, might resent the imputation of parentage.

IV.

WALLENSTEIN—THE ENIGMA OF
HISTORY

IV.

WALLENSTEIN—THE ENIGMA OF HISTORY.

"THE enigma of history," thus we have styled him, though the title " Father of German unity," or again, " Father of grand strategy," would have been equally just—that is, if we can associate so homely a word as " father " with that cold unemotional mind, so utterly detached from the instincts and prejudices of normal humanity, soaring to a purely intellectual atmosphere too rarefied for ordinary minds to breathe.

How little is commonly known of this greatest of politico-military adventurers, who rose to a power only surpassed in modern history by Napoleon, and without the aid of any spring-board of opportunity such as the French revolution afforded the great Corsican. In Germany, admittedly, " Der Friedlander " is a national hero, a common figure of romance and drama, enshrined for posterity in Schiller's immortal verse. Strange that the national hero

in each case should be an alien—for France a
Corsican, for Germany a Czech.

But to Englishmen, what does the name of
Wallenstein convey ?   Usually little more than
a vague association with the laying waste of
Germany in a barbarous struggle inspired by
perverted religion, summed up in some such
phrase as "the atrocities of Tilly and Wallenstein."   Even in the volumes of the 'Ency-
clopædia Britannica' but a bare page and a
half are devoted to the most unique and many-
sided character in modern history, a man who
in a mystery-loving world stands out as the
most unfathomable of all human puzzles.

His very appearance breathed mystery, out-
doing Cassius, "tall, spare, and sallow ; with
small, but quick, penetrating dark eyes.   A
cold, stern, even repulsive earnestness was ever
fixed upon his high gloomy brow ; and nothing
but his boundless profusion and liberality kept
the trembling crowd of attendants round him."
Haughty and reserved, sparing of speech as he
was ready with his pen, Wallenstein, as the
memoirs of Richelieu tell us, "by his sole presence, and the severity of his silence, seemed
to make his soldiers understand that, according
to his usual custom, he would recompense them
or chastise them."

If a stern master—there is a certain resemblance to Wellington in his method and manner of command,—he was an exceptionally generous and discerning one. Count Gualdo, who as an Imperial adherent was certainly not biassed in his favour, tells us : " Actions of spirit and enterprise were sure to meet with his approbation, even when bordering on extravagance. Wit, promptness, and originality were passports to his favour ; but the qualities he valued most were pride, ambition, daring, and resolution. He had a marked aversion to regular court jesters as well as buffoons of every kind ; he was rarely seen to laugh ; but men of genius and talent were sure of his friendship and protection. He was a firm friend to the soldiers, and never lost an opportunity of speaking in their favour. In rewarding or promoting officers, he was guided solely by merit, and never influenced by family connections, or by recommendations from men of rank, not even by those of the Emperor himself."

Several anecdotes survive to show the way in which he gained his hold on the vast and heterogeneous armies of mercenaries who flocked wherever and whenever his banner was raised. Isolani, a leader of light horse, rewarded by 4000 crowns for a feat of arms, lost it in gambling the same night at Wallenstein's quarters, whereupon a page at once placed 2000 ducats before

him. On running to the General's apartment
to thank him for such generosity, Wallenstein
merely pointed to a report just received of the
movement of a Swedish convoy. Isolani took
the hint, gathered his men, and set forth to
capture it. Another time Wallenstein issued
the order that only red sashes were to be worn ;
a young officer instantly tore off an embroidered
sash that he had proudly worn and trampled
it underfoot. Wallenstein, hearing of this act,
promoted him for his spirit of discipline. Again,
out riding one day, a soldier, caught pillaging,
was brought before him. " Hang up the wretch,"
was Wallenstein's curt order, whereupon the man
drew his sword, and calling out, " If I am to
die, I shall at least die guilty," rushed at the
General. He was instantly disarmed—but
pardoned also.

Before passing on to his career, it is advisable
briefly to sketch the immediate origins of the
Thirty Years' War, the background for his
meteoric passage across the stage of history.
Fundamentally a clash between Protestantism
and Catholicism—and the political motives in-
terwoven with the religious threads,—its interminable and kaleidoscopic course was made
possible, if not inevitable, by the disunity of
Germany, the loose and ill-defined framework
of the Empire.

A conglomeration of principalities, of vastly different size and power, over whom the Emperor exercised but a nominal authority, its natural defects were made worse by the fact that on the death of the Emperor his successor was elected by the vote of seven of the greatest princes, termed Electors, three religious and four temporal. Apart, therefore, from the resources of his own State, his control depended on the acquiescence of the other States, and on how far he succeeded in playing off some against the others.

The first phase of this politico-religious struggle was terminated by the Convention of Passau in 1552 and the Augsburg Treaty of religious pacification springing from it, but, like all attempts to stabilise " things as they are," to set fixed bounds to nations and tendencies that grow and change, it was foredoomed to failure. South Germany was the cockpit of the contending interests. Here, in 1607, a religious riot in Donauwörth caused this free city to be deprived of its privileges in brutal manner, and annexed by Catholic Bavaria. The other free cities, taking alarm, formed with certain princes the Protestant Union, for mutual defence, to which in opposition sprang up the Catholic League under the Elector of Bavaria. The two parties faced each other wrangling for nine years, when the smouldering fire burst in a blaze. The actual outbreak came in Bohemia, where the Emperor Mathias, after obtaining the crown by a mixture of fraud and force, sought to break the charter of Bohemian Protestantism granted by his predecessor, Rudolph. On the 23rd May 1618, the commissioners were pitched from the windows of Prague Castle by an irate crowd of Bohemian representatives. It was the signal for the Thirty Years' War, that was to leave Germany little better than a desert, to reduce its population from sixteen millions to little more than four, to destroy as many as thirty thousand villages.

Albrecht Eusebius Wenzeslaus of Waldstein, better known in history as Wallenstein, was born at Herrmanic in Bohemia on the 15th of September 1583. His parents were Protestants, and far from wealthy or highly placed, factors that make his amazing success the more astonishing in an age and an empire where heredity was almost the only key to higher position. Perhaps, however, in his Protestant origin and upbringing we can trace the partial clue to his subsequent attitude of toleration in an age of religious bitterness without parallel in history. As a boy, we are told that he was averse to study—a not unknown feature in the biographies of successful men,—of ungovernable temper, and fond only of military games. There is a very general, and well-based, distrust of the boyhood anecdotes of great men ; the legends that cluster round their early days bear such marked resemblances as to suggest the manufactured product. But one such story of Wallenstein perhaps deserves mention ; that when rebuked one day by an uncle for speaking more in the tone of a prince than the son of mere gentlefolk, the youthful Albrecht retorted, " If I am not a prince, I may yet live to become one." The phrase may have been paralleled countless times, the achievement rarely.

An orphan before he reached his teens, the boy passed under the care first of one uncle and then of another, the second, a Catholic, placing him in a college established by the Jesuits. His conversion, baited by the promise of a release from Latin studies, proved no difficult matter.

Later an arrangement was made for him to accompany a young and wealthy noble who was setting out on a foreign tour, visiting in turn France, Spain, Germany, England, Holland, and Italy. Apart from its broadening influence on Wallenstein during his receptive years, the tour is of interest mainly because Peter Verdungo, the mathematician and astrologer, accompanied the party, from which

we can probably date Wallenstein's famed devotion to the mysterious and speculative science.
Thus in Italy, for whose people he ever entertained contempt, he made a long stay in order
to pursue at Padua his study of astrology. If
it be thought strange that any one whose later
career proved him so immeasurably above the
prejudices and mental limitations of his age,
should dabble in this discredited realm of study,
it is worth recalling that astrology not only
exercised a fascination for the rulers of the
time, but also for the most progressive minds
of seventeenth century science. Keppler, the
great astronomer, was such a devotee, and
" acquired more fame for his accurate forecast
of the Emperor Mathias's death than for his
discovery of the independent motion of the
heavenly bodies." If scientific discovery has
robbed us of this belief in astrology, we must
concede that a strange yet undeniable exaltation
exists in the idea that our destinies might be
linked with the stars—the human palm, so
popular in modern days, is far less inspiring
and more prosaic. Further, if Wallenstein was
really guided in his actions by these celestial
omens, the excellence of their counsel must be
recognised.

From Padua, spurred on by the prospects
thus foretold for him, he went to join the Imperial

army then warring with the Turks. His early hopes of a rapid rise to fame were soon dashed by the hard discovery that the door to high promotion is rarely unlocked save to those who possess the keys of influence or money. He had served several campaigns before he even rose to command a company of infantry.

One chance opened, only to close with speed. His brother-in-law, the celebrated Count Zerotin, recommended him as chamberlain to the Archduke Mathias. Zerotin, in whom candour and truth, rare bed-fellows, were for once synonymous, frankly avowed in this request that it was in order "that his kinsman may have a ladder by which to ascend to fortune." But Wallenstein, whose dislike of subordination and air of natural superiority, genuine but none the less irritating to superiors in rank only, was never cast for the rôle of courtier, and apparently fell foul of the archduke, from which time may date Wallenstein's well-known dislike of courts and their parasites.

This route to fortune barred, Wallenstein found an alternative in the "feminine" ladder, by which many another soldier in history's roll has climbed.

By the advice of friends, he paid his addresses to a wealthy widow, far from young, and already betrothed to another and more highly placed candidate for her fortune. Wallenstein proved himself a more able lover than he had been a courtier, so able that he not only won her, but retained her affection to such a degree that lest his regard might wane she administered a love potion, which caused him a long and severe illness.

As she was much given to such drugs and magical incantations, it was fortunate for his career that the lady died soon after, and left him in undisturbed possession of her extensive property.

When this event occurred Wallenstein was still only twenty-three. Knowing his ambition, and that he had now the means to further it, we should expect the next few years to be fruitful of achievement.

Instead, history loses sight of him completely for ten years. Apparently he lived unobtrusively on his Moravian estates, a circumstance that in one of his ambitious and forceful temperament can only suggest that his breach with the Archduke, now the Emperor, Mathias had been serious.

His reappearance on the stage took place in 1617, when the Archduke Ferdinand, the Emperor to be, was engaged in a minor campaign with Venice. Wallenstein raised a body of two hundred cavalry at his own expense, and went to help his future sovereign. It was a singularly featureless campaign, so that an exploit of Wallenstein's, evading the blockade of Granitza and getting supplies into the fortress, focussed disproportionate attention on him. Against a dull background even the smallest patch of colour stands out, and we recall how Marshal Saxe also owed his first footing on the ladder of military renown to a similar instance of a minor feat being magnified in a drab campaign. But Wallenstein also realised that the easiest and quickest path into the esteem of royal amateurs of war and traditional military authorities is by the appeal to the eye rather than to the mind. The " polish and pipeclay " school is not yet extinct, and it is easier for the mediocre intelligence to become an authority on buttons than on tactics.

To this common trait Wallenstein had the insight to appeal, and the magnificent way in which his men were equipped and clad, the lavish hospitality he dispensed—out of his late wife's fortune,—spread his renown and enhanced his military achievements.

The fame of such an officer was not long in attracting the attention of the Imperial court, whither, on Ferdinand's instigation, he was called, and past indiscretions overlooked. The Emperor made him a count, and gave him a

chamberlain's key as well as command of the
Moravian militia—a position of high trust in an
age so troubled and an Empire so loosely knit.

Strange comment on the way of the world,
the doors which had remained fast locked to
his unsupported merit, were now flung wide
open once he was endowed with the magic
key of wealth. He improved the occasion by
marrying again, this time the daughter of Count
Harrach, the Imperial Minister. This brought
him further wealth and, more important now,
influence as well. Of his domestic life we know
little, save that his choice was guided not by
beauty, but by more solid assets.

It was at this favourable juncture for him
that the affront to the Imperial commissioners
at Prague precipitated civil war. The Bohemians
endeavoured to win him over, but he made
clear his intention to support the Emperor,
using both his influence and force to keep the
Moravians faithful to their allegiance. In this
he failed, and the indignant States decreeing
his expulsion from command, he was forced
to evacuate Olmütz and fall back on Vienna.
However, with his habitual foresight, he took
the precaution to carry away the public treasure
with him and hand it over to the Emperor,
part being given back to him to raise a regiment
of cuirassiers.

In the ensuing war he took a prominent if subordinate part. The Emperor Mathias died at the beginning of the struggle, and Ferdinand succeeded to the vast but troubled heritage of the House of Austria. At a time when Ferdinand's position was critical, it was Wallenstein's capture of the Bohemian wagon fortress at the battle of Rablat that decided the fate of the day, and very probably of the Emperor. For Count Thurn at the head of the Bohemian army was at the gates of Vienna, and Bethlen Gabor with a Hungarian army was marching to join him, when the news arrived of the victory at Rablat, over Count Mansfeld, and of the victor's move on Prague, the Bohemian capital. The Bohemians instantly broke up their camp, and hastened back to defend their own land.

Even after Breitenfeld the situation did not look more menacing for the Empire, and we may speculate whether, but for this feat of Wallenstein in a minor action, the tide of Protestantism might not have swept over the greater part of Europe. The most decisive battles are rarely the greatest in scale, and thus once more we see how trifling causes lead to great events, changing the channels of the world's history.

The respite thus procured enabled Ferdinand to consolidate his position and secure his election as Emperor—a moral factor of importance, for it established the opposition as rebels in the eyes of other sovereigns, though it did not prevent the Bohemians from formally renouncing their allegiance and choosing Frederick, Elector of the Palatinate and son-in-law of James I. of England, as their king.

Imminent danger now threatened the Emperor from another direction, for Bethlen Gabor, pretender to the throne of Hungary, advanced from the east to the outskirts of Vienna, defeating the Imperial general Bucquoi. Again Wallenstein stepped into the breach ; by holding the approaches to the Danube bridge until the Imperial army had retreated across it, and then breaking it down, he staved off the menace. Bethlen Gabor, unable to maintain himself in a ravaged countryside, and with his allies already gone, abandoned his plans and retired.

Freed of this threat from the east, Ferdinand was able to concentrate against Frederick and the Bohemians, and having found an ally in the Elector Maximilian of Bavaria, the combined forces penetrated into the heart of Bohemia, where at the bloody and historic battle of the White Hill, near Prague, the Bohemian forces were routed, and the ill-fated Frederick, absent from the battle listening to a sermon, lost his throne. The proscriptions that followed were reminiscent of a Sulla, nor were they limited to the leading rebels. Massacres and expulsions reached their climax in the decree that all who did not embrace the Catholic faith were to quit the kingdom, and no less than 30,000 families emigrated rather than change their religion.

Wallenstein, who had been engaged elsewhere at the moment of the "White Hill," was despatched into Moravia immediately after, but met no resistance. He reoccupied his estates, which had been confiscated during the rebellion, and seized the chance to buy up many of the confiscated lands of the rebels, thus creating the huge reservoir of wealth that proved so great a factor in his subsequent career.

For a time the process was interrupted by another call for his military services. Bethlen Gabor, with a large army, part Turkish and part Transylvanian, had attempted another invasion, and overthrown the two leading Imperial generals Bucquoi and Dampierre, who both fell in the attempt to resist his progress. But in Wallenstein he met his master, and after two defeats, renounced his claim to the Hungarian throne and made peace. However, two years later, in 1623, he made yet another attempt, and again Wallenstein had to be called in to save the Imperial forces from destruction.

For these great services to the Empire he was
created Duke of Friedland, with the right of
striking coin and granting patents of nobility.
Thus his boyhood's dream had come true, and
with it a further lever to raise money. But
even with the two fortunes he had acquired
by marriage, and their expansion in these other
ways, it remains one of the problems of history
how Wallenstein acquired the seven million
florins we know he paid for the possession of
some sixty confiscated estates.

Then for two years we see another facet of
Wallenstein's many-sided character—he becomes
a model ruler and landowner, a rôle for which
few would have cast this saturnine adventurer,
of restless ambition and vast political schemes.
Turning from destructive to constructive work,
with a rapidity and ease that leaves us breathless,
we find him working out schemes, and personally
supervising their many petty details, by which
to develop his new principality as well as his
own estates, and to improve the lot of their
inhabitants. Not that he loved details, but
he saw the necessity of training others to carry
out his methods when greater affairs should
call him.

He encourages industry and farming, going
even into their technicalities in his orders as
to draining, planting, and breeding cattle. A

great horse-lover, he forms a vast stud, and his letters show considerable veterinary knowledge.

Education is another hobby ; he is constantly advocating its value, and establishes schools broadcast. Building and road-making are others of his concerns, and he uses his wealth to obtain the best architects and artisans from foreign countries. More notable still, perhaps, he voluntarily gave a charter to his subjects which contained extensive rights and privileges. All this in a country so wild as Moravia shows him as a true pioneer of civilisation.

Unique also in his toleration, toning down as far as possible the Emperor's fanatical religious decrees—" Give the peasantry plenty of time," " Do not press the lower orders too hard about religion." Another time he saves a poor widow from the confiscation of her property because she would not change her religion.

This peaceful phase of his career was interrupted by the opening of the second act of the Thirty Years' War, when Christian of Denmark, urged on by the envoys of James I. and their financial promises, entered the German arena as the new champion of the Protestant States. For a while the Emperor opposed Christian and the allied States through the medium of Maximilian of Bavaria and the

Catholic League, the armies being under the command of Tilly. Though not altogether content with this Moses-like rôle of his hands being supported by others, Ferdinand lacked the resources and troops to take an active part. It was then that Wallenstein stepped into the breach, his uncanny vision inspiring him to a stroke of genius, and made the audacious offer to raise and equip an army of 50,000 men. Some poured ridicule on the fantastic proposal, savouring rather of the Arabian Nights than of sober possibility ; others, better understanding his extraordinary capacity, feared the result of allowing a man so ambitious to wield such unique power. Keen though the Emperor was to exert a direct influence on the struggle, he had qualms as to the result, and wished to limit Wallenstein's proposed force to half the strength. To this Wallenstein replied that " twenty thousand men would die of hunger, whereas fifty thousand would enable him to levy requisitions as he wished," and this argument combined with the Emperor's need to gain his agreement. Wallenstein was allowed to nominate his own officers, and in his commission was styled General for the first time. The event proved that Wallenstein had not miscalculated his own influence or the wide fame that his liberality and care for his troops had earned him throughout the fraternity of mercenary soldiers. From far and near soldiers of fortune flocked to enlist under his standard—Poles, Croats, Germans, Walloons, Spaniards. He asked no questions as to religion or race, only that they should be of soldierly mettle, and within a month he had 20,000 men under arms. With this force he prepared to take the field, but even so ere he reached the frontiers of Saxony it had risen to 30,000. The youth who less than twenty years before had been forced to wait for command of a company until he won it by gallantry in default of the money for purchase, and whose prospects of further promotion had appeared the slenderest, had now by the magic of his name achieved what his sovereign, the Emperor, was powerless to do.

True, it would seem as if Wallenstein must have miscalculated, not his influence, but his immediate resources, for we are told that the men were mostly in rags, grumbling for lack of pay, the cavalry wretchedly mounted and worse armed; yet within a brief while their splendour was the admiration of Europe.

Entering the theatre of war, Wallenstein took care to keep at a distance from Tilly, though in communication, having no intention that his exploits should enhance the credit of a rival.

The advent of this new factor disposed the Danish king to open negotiations for peace, but Wallenstein's terms were so dictatorial and unconditional as to prevent any chance of acceptance—a contingency, one suspects, that would have ill consorted with his schemes.

The war continued, unmarked by decisive events, the difficulty of supplies and mutual jealousy apparently preventing the junction of Tilly and Wallenstein for a concentrated blow. This problem of supplies was one common to the armies of the age until Gustavus developed a system of magazines, and was indeed the greatest barrier on purposeful strategy and unswerving maintenance of the strategic object. Like locusts the armies settled in a district, devouring its resources in a wasteful and haphazard fashion, which compelled them to disperse to live instead of concentrating to fight, to move on repeatedly to fresh areas to the detriment of the strategic purpose.

Wallenstein's letters show that he tried hard to remedy this defect, directing his agent in Bohemia to forward corn or even flour, boots and shoes " carefully tied together, pair and pair, in order to prevent mistakes in distribution," cloth, arms, and powder. His own vassals are to have the preference in making and supplying these

articles, and are to be paid in ready money—
the model landlord still. When Wallenstein
himself is in debt, he constantly urges prompt
payment to his creditors, because his far-sighted
judgment tells him that there is no greater
danger to his schemes than that of losing his
credit.

Another incident throws a significant light
on the man and his sublime egotism—he orders
coin to be struck, and is most explicit about the
die; he cannot understand how his agent should
have thought of putting "Dominus protector
meus," as *his* motto is "Invita Invidia."

Throughout the campaign he is seen maintaining a constant correspondence, sometimes
as many as twenty-five letters a day in his own
hand, dealing with the governance and development of his duchy and personal estates. During
a year of famine he orders the poor of the former
to be supplied with bread at a reduced price;
another time it is to establish a silk industry;
again, to build extra powder mills.

Among all his letters that survive not one is
addressed to his wife, yet in his letters he always
refers to her with affection, and from hers it
would seem clear that his behaviour towards
her was considerate and kind.

His one notable military success was against

Count Mansfeld, one of the most remarkable of all soldiers of fortune, and is worth recording because in it we find the genesis of modern camouflage. Wallenstein had fortified a bridgehead on the Elbe, which Count Mansfeld attacked. Foiled, he prepared to repeat his attack, and Wallenstein, aware of this, had the bridge hung over with sails, under the concealment of which he passed his whole army over unobserved, and fell upon Mansfeld, who was routed with a loss of some nine thousand men.

If Wallenstein does not compare with Gustavus as a military reformer, nor in his execution of the material elements of warfare—hitting, guarding, and moving,—he would seem to have a greater appreciation of the moral weapon, as in this rare gem of surprise, and even more in his strategy, as we shall show later.

Soon after, he was called back hurriedly to Austria, threatened once again by Bethlen Gabor, a danger, however, averted by a truce such as the latter made a habit of when in difficulties. Wallenstein seized the opportunity to reform and equip his army in superb style, bringing up its numbers to 40,000 men for the campaign of 1627.

The contrast between his efficient and speedy

methods and those normally the case is best portrayed in Schiller's immortal drama :—

> " Never shall I forget—seven years ago,
> When to Vienna I was sent, to obtain
> Remounts of horses for our cavalry,
> How from one ante-chamber to another,
> They turned me round and round, and left me standing
> Beneath the threshold, ay, for hours together.
> At last a Capuchin was sent to me ;
> I thought, God wot, it must be for my sins.
> Not so ; but this, sir, was the man with whom
> I was to drive a bargain for my horses.
> I was compelled to go with nothing done ;
> And in three days the Duke procured for me
> What in Vienna thirty failed to gain."

While Wallenstein was preparing for this fresh effort, the Protestant States were talking of peace, and in their counsels the ultra-modern reasoning, identical with the 1927 vintage, was heard, that the expense of maintaining armed forces exceeded the possible benefits of their protection : " Let us behave with justice to all men, and all men will behave with justice towards us."

The result of this idealistic pacifism was seen in the feeble resistance that Wallenstein met next spring. Brandenburg, Mecklenburg, Pomerania, despite their plaintive assurances of perfect neutrality, were rapidly overrun and eaten up, Wallenstein scornfully disregarding these entreaties with the remark that " the time had arrived for dispensing altogether with electors, and that Germany ought to be governed, like France and Spain, by a single and absolute sovereign."

He threw the Danes out of Germany and even out of the Jutland peninsula, his progress only stopped by the sea when the king and the remnants of his army had found shelter in the islands. It was an individual triumph—he had taken care that Tilly should be sent to watch the Dutch frontier—but one easily earned, for rare were the instances of a resistance such as Major Dunbar with four companies of Scottish troops put up at the castle of Breitenburg against a whole army—a page of British history that should be for ever memorable.

On the Protestant countryside of Germany the hordes of Wallenstein settled like locusts, and Wallenstein, " the princes' scourge and soldiers' idol," made the war support itself to the benefit of his troops and the misery of the cowardly or idealistic States, now bitterly to repent in tears of blood their neglect to take measures of defence. If Wallenstein took no benefit from the exactions and plundering of his subordinates, he asked and obtained the transfer to himself of the Duchy of Mecklenburg from its hereditary rulers. To refuse such a

boon to the man who had raised the Emperor,
seven years back penned in his palace, to absolute authority from the Adriatic to the Baltic
was difficult, even had his arguments not been
backed by an inconvenient account of three
million florins, arrears for the upkeep of his
armies; in pledge for this unlikely payment
the duchy passed to him.

It was at this brilliant moment that the
shadow of Sweden fell athwart his path, due to
the truce just made between Sweden and Poland.
Did astrological omen or mere foresight warn
him of the menace in the rising star of Gustavus? Wallenstein writes to Arnheim to "keep
a sharp look-out." "We shall certainly have
the Swedes landing on the coast of Mecklenburg or Pomerania." Again, "Gustavus
Adolphus is a dangerous guest, who cannot
be too closely watched."

The wide genius of the man is well shown
in his appreciation of the value of sea-power,
and the efforts, hampered by many difficulties,
he makes to establish a fleet in time to gain
command of the Baltic and foil the Swedish
plans.

To do this he must control the Baltic seaports,
and of these the Hanseatic port of Stralsund
is a key position. To his demand to occupy
it, the citizens, overruling the Senate, returned

a stubborn refusal, and after vain negotiations, Wallenstein had to fall back on military measures. An early assault nearly succeeded, but then the arrival of Swedish help, led by David Leslie, stiffened the resistance. Even so, an armistice had been arranged and terms of submission were being drawn up, when a Danish fleet appeared off the port and infused fresh spirit into the defenders. Though the assaults were renewed, downpours of rain that swamped his trenches and camp compelled Wallenstein to raise the siege.

A memorandum to the Emperor about this time reveals in Wallenstein, the sixteenth century product of an inland empire, a better grasp of the value of sea-power and the possibilities of amphibious warfare than in some twentieth century statesmen of these sea-girt and sea-dependent isles. "They can attack us on all points with superior strength. No army can be imagined sufficiently numerous to guard every accessible part of the coast against landings ; and scattered detachments may be cut up in detail by an enemy who is inaccessible . . . and whose naval operations can neither be followed nor observed by land forces alone." Wallenstein understood that victorious fleets quadruple the strength of armies, that force in war is "mass multiplied by speed," and that sea-mobility is the key to concentration at a vulnerable point to gain a vital point.

Soon after, peace was concluded with Denmark, restoring her former possessions for a pledge of no further interference in the affairs of the Empire. Terms so favourable were probably due to Wallenstein's wish to have his hands free for the greater menace he perceived in Gustavus. To Wallenstein now fell the lot of putting into force the momentous and ill-advised Edict of Restitution, a rôle that inevitably swelled the volume of complaints already aroused by the havoc and exactions of his armies, and so prepared the way for the machinations of his numerous enemies, who disliked his arrogance or feared his power.

"There seems to have been something about the man that awed and repelled minor spirits. His lofty imaginings had no communion with them; and they believed his gloomy look and haughty reserve could indicate only a guilty mind, brooding over dark and dangerous projects." Foremost among his opponents was Maximilian of Bavaria, the second prince of the Empire, and he was supported by the other Electors, for no injury rankles more deeply than a slight to man's pride.

At the Diet of Ratisbon in 1630 a long catalogue of charges against him was drawn up,

and we notice that the burden of the princes'
grievance comes before the more specific ones
of their subjects : "Wallenstein, a man of
restless and ferocious spirit, has without the
consent of the States . . . obtained absolute
power in every part of the Empire. And he uses
this power as if he, the mere nobleman, were
the lord and director of princes, and they only
his servants and subordinates." Of the tribu-
lation wrought by his army there is no question,
but the evidence shows that Wallenstein strove
to repress these excesses, and the severity of
his punishments against pillagers were as famous
as his lavish rewards. But in an army lacking
any regular system of discipline, and bound
solely by mercenary ties, in which no chain
of responsibility existed, the efforts of one man
could have little effect beyond his immediate
purview. All the crimes of his troops, however,
were laid at his door, and it is likely that his
attempts to repress these helped to undermine
the very bastion on which he depended against
his princely enemies. To these were added
the enmity of foreign powers like Spain and
France, who feared to see the Emperor's might
and sway extended, and realised full well that
Wallenstein was the power that buttressed the
Imperial throne. Thus Richelieu, at the very
moment when he was concluding an alliance

with Gustavus, played a main part, by subtle intrigue, to remove the chief obstacle in the path of his new and secret ally.

Unhappily for Wallenstein, the very completeness of his triumph paved the way for his removal. When the need for protection disappears with the abolition of the danger, men and nations quickly forget the sense of obligation—to which truth the lessons of the American colonies and Egypt testify in our own history.

The horizon seemed clear, for the Emperor did not share Wallenstein's apprehensions about " the new little army " in the north, and weak sovereigns often feel jealous of their powerful subjects. Ferdinand, perhaps less unwillingly than he pretended, yielded to the appeal of the princes and of Richelieu's agent, and sent envoys to inform Wallenstein of his removal from command.

Such a message to a man at the head of an army of 100,000 men, owing no allegiance to any one but their commander, raised speculation as to whether he would disregard it. " It was singular," men said, " that the Emperor should obey the Electors ; but it would be more singular still should the General obey the Emperor."

To the world's surprise, Wallenstein accepted this decision calmly and pleasantly, treating the envoys with the greatest courtesy and princely hospitality. Producing an astronomical calculation, he said to them, " You may observe by the planets that the spirit of Maximilian predominates over the spirit of Ferdinand ; I can attach no blame to the Emperor therefore, though I regret that he should have given me up so easily ; but I shall obey." The dignity and serenity with which he received so bitter a blow compels our admiration. Did the secret of this attitude lie in a more than human wisdom, able to look to the future even in face of the apparent ruin of his life's work, to give no vent to natural indignation such as might raise an obstacle to his recall ? Or was it part of that extraordinary combination of boundless ambition with philosophical detachment that makes his character and purpose more difficult to fathom than almost any other great man, the enigma of history indeed.

In none of the letters he writes at this period is there the least trace of resentment against his Imperial master. The curtain drops on the commander of vast armies, and rises once again on the model feudal lord, absorbed in the thousand details of an estate. The transformation is so sudden, so startlingly complete that, sitting in the stalls of history, we are inclined, unjustly, to suspect a stage trick. At Gitchin in retirement the pomp and state of a king surrounded him—a splendour that would be flamboyant was it not in keeping with the spirit of the times and a frame for a personality of natural grandeur.

Six gates led to his palace, twelve patrols circled continuously round his habitation to keep every noise at a distance, sixty pages attended him, Imperial chamberlains resigned office to enter his service, on his travels his attendants filled a hundred carriages, and his court accompanied him in sixty state coaches. His palace at Sagan would have been one of the wonders of the world had he lived to see it completed. Yet he himself took little part in the brilliant feasts and functions of his court, convivial pleasures had no appeal, and Wallenstein spent his hours in ceaseless work. A man purely mind, devoid apparently of either emotions or senses, he used this magnificence merely as an instrument. He might be termed indeed the founder of modern advertising science. Yet for flattery he has a supreme contempt. The attendant who declared that everybody regards him as the greatest general the world has ever seen is dismissed; another who says that he is called the great Bohemian beast is rewarded for his candour. A few men of humble birth have risen to equal power in times of revolution, none surely by the orthodox channels of a monarchical state—Wallenstein was the power beside the throne, not merely behind it.

It is the way of small minds to suppose in others the revengeful feelings they would themselves harbour if slighted, and it was but natural that those who had brought about Wallenstein's overthrow should imagine him plotting in retirement dark schemes of reprisal. With a man so sombre and reserved, such rumours multiplied, and the seeds were sown that bore fruit in the tragedy of Eger.

Tilly sends him, "out of friendship and affection," some French newspapers containing reports that he had received an envoy of Gustavus, to which Wallenstein replies that "he is not surprised by the reports circulated at his expense, such having been the world's good fashion from time immemorial; and as to the papers they are amusing to read, though best answered by being laughed at. The open town of Gitchin, situated in the midst of the Austrian dominions, is not a place wherein to form dangerous projects." He passes on the papers to Vienna with, as comment, the Spanish proverb, which, translated, reads, "The rogue believes every man to be of his own stamp."

Wallenstein bided his time, not for revenge, but for the recall his clear brain perceived to be inevitable. The legend of his treasonable designs, sedulously fostered by his enemies and by an Imperial court anxious to justify its base ingratitude, has gained acceptance in history. Yet it is difficult to reconcile either with his letters or the far-sighted and gratuitous advice he tendered the Emperor, from his retirement, on the conduct of the war. This advice embodied a plan that marks Wallenstein a master of grand strategy. It was to win over as an ally the King of Denmark, and then employ his fleet to gain command of the Baltic, striking at Gustavus's communications with Sweden, his Achilles heel. Here was the alleged traitor making his sovereign a freewill offering of a plan that would have paralysed the Swedish advance !

The Emperor, delighted, asks Wallenstein to initiate negotiations, the way for which had been paved by the moderation of the earlier terms of peace. We know that Christian of Denmark fell in with the proposal, and that the treaty was on the verge of being signed. Why it was never completed is a mystery, though the obvious explanation lies in the Imperial reverses in the theatre of war. " Of all sciences diplomacy is surely the weakest and most inefficient ; it is, in fact, nothing more than the slave of military success, depending entirely on the force, ready in the background, to give weight to protocols."

What a change had occurred since Wallenstein's dismissal—the Imperial armies dispersed, the enemy on the Danube! Space forbids a relation of these events, already surveyed in the study of Gustavus Adolphus. Suffice to recall that with the opening of the campaign of 1632 the Swedish Army crossed the Danube to overrun Bavaria, while the Saxons invaded Bohemia, the gateway to Vienna.

While Gustavus had been conquering province after province, the one man capable of opposing him had been building towns and schools, and planting the domestic arts in the wilds of Bohemia. Another dramatic change of scene, and Wallenstein is once more the " creator of vast armies."

The Imperial Minister, Questenberg, writes as a suppliant to beg his aid : " We now see our error plainly enough ; and as the miracles we anticipated have not come to pass, we would gladly retrace our steps, if we only knew how."

The requests multiply, but Wallenstein holds firm, alleging severe gout as his excuse, until at last the Emperor writes in his own hand, entreating the man he had dismissed " not to forsake him in the hour of adversity."

Wallenstein gives way, though a hitch occurs

when he hears that it is proposed he should share the command with an Emperor's son. Scornfully he declares, "Never will I accept a divided command—no, not even were God Himself to be my colleague in office. I must command alone, or not at all." The point at once yielded, he agrees to take command, or rather to raise an army, for there was none to command. But he stipulates that his tenure shall be only for three months, when he will retire and leave the Emperor to dispose of the command as he wishes.

The magic of his name sufficed. Soldiers of fortune flocked from every corner of Europe, and within the time an army of 40,000 men was assembled, raised largely at his own expense and fully equipped.

But the Imperial court knew well that Wallenstein's name was the sole tie, and sent envoys to beg him to continue in command. Though his illness was genuine, it is difficult to resist the conclusion that this three months' condition was but a move in the game, a lever whereby to gain his full terms. He asked twenty-four hours for consideration, then delivered them in writing. He was to be commander-in-chief, with absolute power, of all the forces; all rights of appointment, reward, pardon, and confiscation were to be vested in him. The

Emperor and his son were not even to appear with the army, still less to exercise any authority. As a certain reward he was to be given one of the hereditary provinces of the House of Austria, and as extraordinary reward one of the conquered provinces.

So dire was the need that the Emperor swallowed his pride, and agreed, without demur, to these humiliating terms, which meant that Wallenstein became the power *above* the throne —so, as it proved, signing his own death-warrant. Nevertheless, to ascribe these conditions solely to overweening pride would seem unjust. Rather would Wallenstein, the first grand strategist, appear to have grasped the principle of *unity of command*—by none more infringed than Austria throughout its chequered history,—appreciating that to counter Gustavus, the absolute chief of a military monarchy, equal power and freedom of action was essential.

Maximilian begged for aid against the principal enemy, the Swedes in Bavaria, but Wallenstein turned north instead against the Saxons, throwing them out of Bohemia, while simultaneously negotiating to detach the Elector from alliance with Sweden. If by so doing he infringed the canons of present-day military pundits, his was a more far-sighted strategy, for apart from the risk of pitting his new levies against troops

flushed with victory, his double threat to Gustavus's communications and to his chief ally
seized the initiative from the Swedish king,
and compelled the prompt evacuation of Bavaria
more simply and economically than a direct
move.

Before continuing his intended advance into
Saxony, Wallenstein directed Maximilian to quit
Bavaria and join him, with his army, at Eger.
How bitter must this enforced subordination
have been to the Elector, prime instigator of
Wallenstein's dismissal.   At their meeting a
formal reconciliation took place, though it is
remarked that " the Elector was more perfect
in the art of dissimulation than the Duke of
Friedland."

Leaving Bavaria hurriedly, Gustavus attempted to prevent this junction, but, failing,
and faced with a combined army of 60,000
men, fell back on Nuremberg.

Thither Wallenstein followed, and finding the
Swedes entrenched, remarked that " battles
enough had been fought already, and it was
time to try another method."   With this aim
he occupied and fortified a position near the
city by which he could command Gustavus's
lines of supply with his Croat light horse, ideal
troops for the purpose.   This object of starving
his rival out he maintained unswervingly, deaf

to all challenges of battle from Gustavus, until
at last the Swedish king, shadowed by the
gaunt spectre of famine, organised a grand
assault on Wallenstein's position. The throw
failed, after desperate efforts on both sides,
and two weeks later Gustavus, yielding to
famine and superior will-power, broke up his
camp and marched away unhindered.

As a soldier, judged by modern standards,
or even by his rival, Wallenstein's lack of vigour
is hardly to his credit, but as a man and a grand
strategist playing for higher stakes than local
military success, his firmness and will in following the course planned out is wholly admirable.
The great Czech is the supreme poker player
of military history. He appreciated full well
that the Swedes had acquired such a moral
ascendancy that to meet them in open battle
was to court defeat, and further that Gustavus's
hold over the German States depended on his
reputation for invincibility.

This, the check at Nuremberg perceptibly
shook in the eyes of Europe ; as Wallenstein
phrased it, " The King has blunted his horns."

It may be remarked that Wallenstein's profound grasp of psychology, perhaps his supreme
faculty, was equally the secret of his influence
with his troops.

Instead of following Gustavus, who had again

moved south on the Danube, Wallenstein turned north and struck once more against Saxony—a master move that again brought Gustavus to heel, and, automatically, prompt relief to Bavaria. For this mistake the Swedish king atoned by a return march so rapid that he caught up Wallenstein near Leipsig, before the Imperial general had been able to bring the Saxon army to battle or intimidate the Elector into a separate peace. Hearing of the Swedish approach, Wallenstein moved back from Leipsig to meet them, but finding Gustavus strongly posted at Naumburg, abstained from any attempt to attack.

As the Swedes were entrenched, Wallenstein concluded no farther advance was imminent, and allowed Pappenheim to march to attack the Moritzburg near Halle, himself standing at Lützen, where he could cover alike this expedition and the approach to Leipsig. But Gustavus, hearing of this dispersion of the enemy, moved unexpectedly to attack Wallenstein.

Caught unprepared and with but 12,000 men at hand, the latter rose to the emergency, sent Isolani's Croats to delay the oncoming Swedes, ordered his various corps to concentrate with all speed, and to Pappenheim despatched this message : "The enemy is marching hither. Break up instantly with every man and gun, so as to arrive early in the morning." Isolani's resistance, even though routed after a time, and the early fall of darkness, saved the Imperial army from attack that day, and by the morrow Wallenstein was drawn up in battle order, with his right on Lützen, parallel to and behind the Leipsig road.   Next morning a thick November fog delayed the opening of battle until nearly noon, while Pappenheim was drawing ever nearer.   It proved a typical parallel battle unmarked by striking manœuvres, fought in a shroud of mist that confused its movements and obscured the record of its incidents.   The initial Swedish attack succeeded on the right, but farther to the left was driven back across the road, and Gustavus, hurrying to rally and lead forward his troops in the centre, met his death.   When the news filtered through, it fired the Swedes to avenge his fall by a supreme fury of assault before which, despite all Wallenstein's efforts, the Imperialists recoiled.   At this critical moment Pappenheim's squadrons restored the balance, and Wallenstein seized the chance to rally and counter-attack with his infantry centre, hurling the Swedes back and regaining the lost ground and guns.   Wallenstein himself bore a charmed life, all his attendants struck down, his spur torn off by a cannon shot, and several musket balls lodging in his coat ;   but Pappenheim fell, dismay spread throughout his troops, and without cavalry to confirm their momentary success, the exhausted infantry, disorganised by their charge, were pushed back in one last final throw by the Swedish second line, still almost intact. The Swedes remained to mourn their king, while under cover of darkness Wallenstein, with his shattered forces, withdrew towards Leipsig, with the loss of his baggage and artillery. So reduced and disorganised was his army that, abandoning Leipsig, he was forced to fall back into Bohemia to recuperate in winter quarters.

Though a military reverse for the Imperialists, the death of Gustavus was a political triumph, dislocating all the Protestant plans. In all Catholic countries the *Te Deum* was sung for the delivery.

During the winter of 1632-33, both sides reformed their forces for a fresh trial, and in Bohemia we find Wallenstein making what appears to be almost the sole tactical reforms of his career—depriving the heavy cavalry of their carbines, and at the same time insisting that they should all be provided with cuirasses "because it was found in the late action that the mail-clad horsemen did their duty, while the others ran away." In this his views, contrary to those of Gustavus, coincide with Saxe's later, embodying the principle which underlies the modern tank—that of combining mobility, protection, and hitting power in each individual fighting entity.

With his army raised again to 40,000, more splendidly equipped than ever, Wallenstein took the field in the spring of 1633, and with his great rival removed, success would seem pre-destined ; the crushing of their opponent was indeed eagerly anticipated at the Imperial court. Instead, we are to see yet another transforma-tion of this extraordinary man. Forsaking the easy and profitable pursuit of military conquest, Wallenstein enters on his last and grandest rôle—that of fathering German unity. The disappearance of Gustavus was treated by him as an opportunity to work for peace. Negotia-tions with the Saxons were his first step, but beyond this his intentions remain one of the enigmas of history. The series of negotiations and intrigues that follow, interspersed with military operations, are far too intricate to trace here. Suffice to say that the general tenor of reports and rumours was that Wallen-stein had offered to join with the Saxons in forcing peace on the Emperor, the Jesuits were to be driven from the Empire, the Protestants to be given religious freedom and their property restored. Whether this common action was to include the Swedes or to expel them also remains in doubt. Arnheim, the Saxon general, we know went to Oxenstierna, the Swedish chancellor, with alleged proposals from Wallenstein, but whether Arnheim had any authority from Wallenstein is doubtful. In Richelieu's words, "the court of Rome had lost in him the most perfect Jesuit that ever lived." From Arnheim's own letters to the Duke of Brandenburg, Wallenstein was urging as a preliminary to peace that the Swedes must be driven out. We know, again, that Richelieu was offering the highest bribes, the Bohemian crown and a million livres a year, if Wallenstein would join with France against the Emperor, yet without result.

These rumours, however, penetrated to Vienna, where his enemies assiduously propagated them, and Wallenstein's spirit of peace and religious toleration increased their animosity, just as his attempts to maintain discipline and prevent plunder antagonised many of his subordinate officers. Another cause of offence arose out of the victory of Steinau, Wallenstein's military masterpiece. Here, drawing the Saxon forces away from the Swedes by a clever feint, he lay concealed by the Lusatian mountains, allowing the Saxons to overtake and pass him. Then, turning suddenly on the Swedes under Count Thurn, he surprised and surrounded them.

Caught unprepared, and given half an hour
to decide, Thurn capitulated on terms that the
officers should be allowed to go free and the
men take service under their captors. But
the court of Vienna had such malice against
their old enemy, Count Thurn, that their chagrin
over his release was not mollified by Wallenstein's witty explanation : " It were well if the
allies had no better general ; and at the head of
the Swedish army he will be of more use to us
than in prison."

Following up this victory with a promptness
such as he had never shown before, and a strategic
insight unparalleled in his age, Wallenstein
swept through Silesia and down the Oder. He
was on the verge of cutting off the Swedes from
the Baltic when recalled by the short-sighted
entreaties of the Emperor and Maximilian,
fearful of the danger to Bavaria. It was just
after this, when Wallenstein was about to go
into winter quarters, that the first ominous
signs of the Emperor's distrust appeared. In
requiring the general to send him a state of
distribution, so that he himself might arrange
the quartering, he hints his dislike that " an
appearance (might be) given to foreign nations
that we possess only divided power in our own
dominions, and have a colleague on the throne."
Soon after, Ferdinand, while maintaining a

friendly correspondence, determined to deprive
Wallenstein of command.

The plot thickened, and the Italian officers,
for whose military qualities and brigandly ways
Wallenstein had often expressed his contempt,
combined with the Spanish and Bavarian elements to work on the Emperor's fears, until,
late in January 1634, Ferdinand sent a secret
commission to Generals Gallas and Piccolomini,
depriving Wallenstein of command and declaring
him an outlaw, to be taken "dead or alive."
The conspirators saw the risk of giving notice
of dismissal to a victorious general at the head
of a great and devoted army, while their greed
was inflamed by the prospect of dividing the
spoil of his vast estates ; the Emperor also
was probably not unwilling to cancel by a single
blow his debt, not merely of gratitude, but
of twenty million florins. Rumours must have
reached Wallenstein, for after calling his officers
together, and signing with them a joint de-
claration of their "entire devotion to the Emperor," he despatched two messengers to the
Emperor to advise him of his readiness to resign
and to appear anywhere to answer any charges.
The messengers, however, were intercepted by
Piccolomini, and when the proclamation of out-
lawry was posted up in Prague, Wallenstein
realised his full danger. He determined to

seek the protection of the allies, and sent a
messenger to the Duke of Weimar to ask for
aid, which, through suspicion of a ruse, was
at first refused—surely proof that he had not
been engaged in treasonable intrigues. Meanwhile Wallenstein, quitting the army, set out
to meet them, with only a small escort of infantry and dragoons, the latter under Colonel
Butler. This Irish officer sent his chaplain
secretly to Piccolomini to inform him of the
move, and to promise aid in frustrating Wallenstein. On the second night, the 24th of February
1634, the party arrived at the frontier fortress
of Eger, held by two Scottish officers, Colonel
Gordon and Major Leslie. To them Wallenstein
told what had happened, and left it to them to
accompany him or not as they thought proper.
Gordon and Leslie agreed to do this, but that
night Butler showed them orders he had received
from Piccolomini, and the three pledged themselves to the murder. Into the conspiracy
Butler brought seven other officers, five Irish-
men and two Spaniards. The next evening
several of Wallenstein's chief adherents were
invited to sup with Gordon in the citadel. The
gates were closed after they had entered, guards
posted to prevent escape, and eighteen dragoons
placed in the rooms adjoining the dining-hall.
But no move was made until the dessert had

been placed on the table and the servants dismissed, when, the signal given, the dragoons rushed out and slew the unarmed guests.

The first act of the tragedy over, the conspirators held a council, at which Gordon made a plea for clemency, but was overruled by Butler. Towards midnight, Butler, followed by Captain Devereux and six Irish dragoons, went to Wallenstein's quarters, the others going upstairs while Butler waited below. It is said that Wallenstein had just dismissed for the night his astrologer, Seni, who had declared that the stars still foretold impending danger. Devereux broke into the room, and Wallenstein, who, aroused by noises, was at the window, turned to meet the assassin. Too proud to parley, dignified to the last, he opened his arms to the blow, and received the thrust of Devereux's halberd through his chest.

To cover this deed of base ingratitude to the man to whom he owed all, the Emperor and his satellites prepared an elaborate account of Wallenstein's " conspiracy " against the Empire, among the many charges being that he had negotiated with Gustavus, and that he " not only employed Protestants in his army, but allowed them free exercise of their religion and estates "— this last true ! Though historians—even German historians, until Doctor Förster a century ago

obtained access to the archives of Vienna—
swallowed this official concoction without query,
the House of Austria knew its weakness, and
sought to bury the affair in oblivion.   When
Frederick the Great asked Joseph II., "How
it really was with that story of Wallenstein,"
the Emperor cryptically replied that "he could
not possibly doubt the honour and integrity of
his ancestor."

But what were the exact plans maturing in
that gigantic brain is, and must remain, one
of the unfathomable problems of history.   Oxenstierna, even, perhaps the best-informed man
and ablest judge of character of the time, declared
long after that he could never comprehend the
object that Wallenstein really had in view.

In the whole of history no parallel exists to
the strange career, and stranger mentality, of
this many-sided genius, compound of Julius
Cæsar, Bismarck, and x—an unknown quantity.
Wallenstein is unique.

Yet through all the mystery surrounding this
man, "whose character," in Schiller's words,
"obscured by faction's hatred and applause,
still floats, unfixed and stationless in history,"
suffice it that we can trace a spirit of toleration
solitary in the welter of the world's bitterest
religious and fratricidal struggle, akin rather
perhaps to the twentieth century than to the

nineteenth century spirit; a striving after the national unity which was to be realised two and a half centuries later; a grasp of the grand strategical truth that military success is not an end in itself, that force is but one instrument of war policy, and that the true object is to ensure a progressive and prosperous continuance of our peace-time policy in after years. "Germany turns ever to Wallenstein as she turns to no other leader of the Thirty Years' War . . . such faithfulness is not without reason. Wallenstein's wildest schemes were always built upon the foundation of Germany's unity. In the way in which he walked that unity was doubtless unobtainable. . . . But during the long dreary years of confusion which were to follow, it was something to think of the last supremely able man whose life had been spent in battling against the great evils of the land, against the spirit of religious intolerance, and the spirit of division."

V.

GENERAL WOLFE—GRANDSIRE OF THE UNITED STATES

1727-1927

V.

GENERAL WOLFE—GRANDSIRE OF THE UNITED STATES.

1727-1927.

AMONG all the meteors that have flashed across the sky of human history, the course of Wolfe was the briefest. For only in 1758 did he shoot above the horizon of public knowledge, and in September 1759 expired—at the age of thirty-two. Yet, unlike the majority of human meteors, the close of his career marked not the end but rather the beginning of his achievement; for whereas the brilliant but solitary military stroke at Quebec might have faded from memory, Wolfe's place in the roll of history is linked with that of the British Empire and enlarges with the growth of the Dominion of Canada—nay, even with that of the United States. For as he founded the one, so he made possible the other.

Nor can it be said that, like Nelson or Lincoln, a dramatic death in the hour of triumph has

enhanced his historical stature, for of all the
famous young cut off in the first flower of their
manhood none had so clearly fulfilled yet un-
fulfilled their promise, none were so obviously
destined, by the time and the opportunity, to
unfold far more their blossoming genius.

We cannot even measure Wolfe's impress on
history by the material result in the New World,
for there was a slower growth than his spiritual
inspiration during the eighteenth century—when
the British Empire was being forged.   He of
all men symbolised most that glorious spell
when " England stood upon a pinnacle of greatness which she had never reached before."   In
Seeley's words, " we have forgotten how, through
all that remained of the eighteenth century,
the nation looked back upon those two or three
splendid years as upon a happiness that could
never return, and how long it continued to be
the unique boast of the Englishman—

'That Chatham's language was his mother-tongue,
 And Wolfe's great name compatriot with his own.'"

But if Wolfe's fame to-day rests in a single
year of achievement and its boundless sequel,
his interest and his value for the student of war
and of human nature lie even more in the earlier
years of striving and preparation for his opportunity.   To youth and age, to the subaltern

and the general, to the public and the politician, Wolfe's story has a message and a moral. This it is our purpose here to uncover.

In this age when a popular interest in the past and easy means of transport have combined to spread the vogue of pilgrimages to the birthplaces of the great, it is strange that Wolfe's is not more known. Every week of summer thousands pass through it, Londoners and visitors to London. But of the vast numbers who know his birthplace, how many know that it is his birthplace? Yet in Westerham itself, nestling near the border between Kent and Surrey, kindly time and pious hands have preserved his memory in almost unique degree, so that the pilgrim may not merely mark the spot where Wolfe was born but move in the same surroundings, and recreate the atmosphere in which his boyhood was spent. For in this old-world village, passed over by the changing hand of time, can still be seen the vicarage in which he was born—by the chance of his mother's labour beginning when on a call there; the Tudor house " Spiers "—later rechristened Quebec House—in which he lived with his parents until he was twelve, when the family moved to Greenwich; and, at the other end of the village, Squerryes Court, the home of his boyhood friend, George Warde, where on a Christmas visit just

before his fifteenth birthday he received his
commission in his father's regiment of Marines.
Young Wolfe was playing in the garden when
the missive came, and on the spot beneath tall
trees stands now a memorial urn and pedestal
thus inscribed :—

> " Here first was Wolfe with martial ardour fired,
> Here first with glory's brightest flame inspired ;
> This spot so sacred will for ever claim
> A proud alliance with its hero's name."

The first line is a poetic hyperbole, for his martial
ardour was an earlier growth. He sprang from
a military and adventurous stock, who had left
England in the fifteenth century to seek their
fortune in Ireland, and Wolfe's great-grandfather
shared so prominently in Limerick's obstinate
resistance to Cromwell's troops that he only
saved his life by escape to Yorkshire, where he
settled. His grandson, Edward, the father of
James Wolfe, distinguished himself in the wars
of Marlborough and the '15 Rebellion, but the
long peace which followed caused a halt in his
progress, and turned his thoughts to domesticity.
It was after his marriage with Henrietta Thomp-
son, of Marsden in Yorkshire, that he settled at
Westerham, and his later change to Greenwich
was apparently due to revived hopes of active
employment when the gathering war-clouds began
to threaten the peace which Walpole had so

long striven to preserve. The move may also have been suggested by the desire to give James and his younger brother, Edward, a better education, for at Greenwich they were fortunate in a schoolmaster, the Rev. Samuel Swinden, of a type then rare, who not only made an imprint on the boys' characters but developed in them a desire for knowledge. But in James martial exploits were a still earlier impression, and when in 1740 the war-drums beat and his father went to join the ill-fated Cartagena expedition, the boy of thirteen and a half, despite his mother's horrified protests, coaxed from his father permission to accompany him as a volunteer. That precocious venture, fortunately for James, took him no nearer to the Spanish Main than the Solent, for illness caused him to be sent ashore before the sailing, and back to his school-books. Better that transitory humiliation than to have shared the horrors of that expedition and the fever, which wrought the death or ruined the health of thousands of more robust and older men, including Laurence Washington, who succumbed some years later to its effects. His fate, as Bradley recalls, left the family estates to George Washington, and thereby gave the future leader of the American colonies the means to assume a public career. The history of the world has

often turned on trifling incidents, and it may
even be that if Wolfe had gone, or Laurence
Washington not gone, to Cartagena, the United
States had not arisen.

With Wolfe pertinacity triumphed, however,
eighteen months later when his commission in
the Marines reached him at Squerryes Court.
Five months later he exchanged into the 12th
Foot (now the Suffolk Regiment), which was
about to sail from Deptford for Flanders. But
riots between the burghers and the soldiery
were all the fighting he saw for a year, and he
was still in quarters at Ghent when his brother,
who was a year younger, joined him early in
1743.   At last in February the army set out
for the Rhine, and although the wintry march
taxed his slight physique, his ardent spirit led
him to take on the extra duties of acting adjutant. Marching through snow up to their knees,
with provisions so short that at times they lived
purely on ammunition bread, and sleeping on
straw, was a hard initiation for two rather
delicate youngsters, and as the roads got worse
they were driven to hire and share a horse between
them. The eagerly desired baptism of fire came
in June at the battle of Dettingen, the last in
which an English King led his troops in person.
A letter from James Wolfe to his father after
the fight reveals this stripling as a candid but

discerning critic. He castigates the Blues for firing their pistols instead of using their superior weight in a charge, and bitingly adds : "Their excuse for retreating—they could not make their horses stand the fire !" As regards the share of his regiment in this infantry clash, he says : "The Major and I (for we had neither colonel nor lieutenant-colonel) were employed in begging and ordering the men not to fire at too great a distance, but to keep it till the enemy should come near us ; but to little purpose. The whole fired when they thought they could reach them, which had like to have ruined us."

Sixteen years later, on the heights of Abraham, Wolfe's doctrine bore fruit in a volley "like a single cannon-shot "—held back until the English troops could see the whites of their enemy's eyes—which by its tremendous and instantaneous effect decided in a single second the battle of Quebec and the fate of Canada. Wolfe's horse was shot during the first attack, and he had to do his adjutant's duties all that day and the next " on foot, in a pair of heavy boots." That his own efforts were more effective than he suggests is shown by him being confirmed as adjutant and promoted lieutenant a few weeks later. It was the first step which marked him out from the common ruck, and, best of all, his behaviour seems to have caught the eye of the

King's son, the Duke of Cumberland. If Wolfe's
father had neither wealth nor patronage, his
services had earned him a certain degree of influence in the army, and the son's early grasp of
the chance of distinction gave the father a
lever for his efforts ; such influence and money
as he possessed were on the whole ungrudgingly
used henceforth to forward his son's career.
Next year James was promoted captain into the
4th Foot (now the King's Own Royal Regiment),
but the pleasure was dimmed by the death of
his brother, too delicate a plant to endure the
wintry rigours of Flanders, and, owing to his
own transfer, the brothers were separated at
the last. Nevertheless the transfer was doubly
fortunate for him, for at the battle of Fontenoy,
which he thus missed, his old regiment was
almost wiped out, and when he arrived with the
reinforcements sent to make good the heavy
loss of the army, the Duke of Cumberland gave
him a vacancy as brigade-major. Fortune,
indeed, favoured him a third time, for a few
weeks after his departure from Ghent, the place
was surprised and the garrison taken. His
next laurels were to come, however, not in
Flanders but in Scotland, for in July, Prince
Charles Edward, the Young Pretender, landed
there for his stroke to regain the lost throne of
the Stuarts. Accompanying the troops recalled

from Flanders to meet this danger, Wolfe had
to fret his soul at Newcastle while the elderly
Marshal Wade, better at road-building than road-
covering, let Prince Charles slip past him and
on to Derby. When the Jacobites in turn lost
their nerve and retired towards Scotland, the
Newcastle force, now under " Hangman Hawley,"
moved north to intercept them, but at Falkirk
was so discomfited by the wild onset of the
Highlanders that they had to retreat from the
field. The Duke of Cumberland now hurried
north to assume the supreme command, and
although his energetic pursuit of the rebel army
was baulked by bad weather, forcing him to
halt at Aberdeen for six weeks, his advance
began again early in April 1746. Its sequel
was the battle of Culloden Moor, which ended
the '45 Rebellion, and finally extinguished the
Stuart hopes.

Upon the Duke's arrival in Scotland, Wolfe
had been made aide-de-camp to Hawley—the
latter's mishandling of Falkirk suggests the
significance,—but although he writes fully upon
both battles he tells us nothing of his own share.
There is, however, scope for reflection on this
contrast between Hawley at Falkirk and at
Culloden, where the dragoons under his command made the decisive charge on the enemy's
flank. An anecdote, told by Sir Henry Stuart

Allanton, but its source uncertain, has come down to us that when the Duke was riding over the battlefield he ordered Wolfe, who was riding with him, to shoot a wounded Highlander who was glaring at them with scornful defiance, and that Wolfe replied : " My commission is at your Highness's disposal, but I never can consent to become an executioner." Even if the story is based on fact, the circumstances would suggest that the order came not from the Duke but from Hawley, whose character it fits.

During the months which followed Culloden, Wolfe had the disagreeable duty of conveying Hawley's orders for the punishment of the rebels. Several letters survive, and while the general's instructions are impersonally and exactly expressed, as becomes a loyal staff officer, there is just a hint that Wolfe had little taste for his commander's ways. He was back again in the Netherlands in 1747, serving under Cumberland, and his conduct at the battle of Laffeldt, where he was wounded, appears to have gained him the official thanks of the Commander-in-Chief. As a result of the wound several months were spent on leave at home, where this veteran of six campaigns celebrated his coming of age. On returning in the following spring he found himself detached to supervise at Breda the assembling of a body of German troops, and in compensation received a private promise from Cumberland of a major's commission for nothing —these were the days of purchase—in a regiment where the lieutenant-colonel was dying. This prospect of jumping up two rungs of the ladder simultaneously was baulked by the early end of this war of the Austrian Succession, as indeterminate in its terms of peace as in its course. Wolfe, instead of resting on his oars and enjoying the relaxation brought by peace, is seized with the idea of broadening his education and horizon by travel ; but he evidently scents a refusal, for he writes to his mother : " There will be difficulties in everything that contradicts a principle or settled opinion, entertained among us, that an officer neither can, nor ought ever to be, otherwise employed than in his particular military functions. If they could beat men's capacities down, or confine their genius to that rule . . . no man would ever be fitted for higher employment than he is in. 'Tis unaccountable that who wishes to see a good army can oppose men's enlarging their notions. . . ." But if this project was still-born, the check on his advancement was not long, and in June 1749 he was gazetted major in the 20th Foot, then Lord George Sackville's, and now the Lancashire Fusiliers. To us it is amusing to find this youth, not yet twenty-two, writing despondently of his prospects during the brief interval of waiting : " Other views and interests succeed at the end of a war, and favours are thrown in quite a different direction " ; and even talking with sarcastic resignation of the prospect of garrison duty " at Gibraltar or Minorca—a very desirable retreat and well adapted to my years and inclination ! "

He was now destined to eight years of peace soldiering ; and although these years were for him infinitely more varied, more productive, and fuller of incident than is the normal soldier's lot, he was chafing all the time at the curb on his lofty ambitions.

His new regiment was in Scotland, and almost at once he became acting commander through the departure of its lieut.-colonel, Edward Cornwallis, to the governorship of Nova Scotia. Wolfe set out on a campaign of improvement, demanding of the captains written notes upon the character of every man in their companies, and telling the subalterns that " a young officer should not think he does too much." The officers are also to watch the looks of the men, and observe " if any are thinner or paler than usual, that the reason may be inquired into and proper means used to restore them to their former vigour." When he ultimately left the regiment it was recognised as " the best-drilled and disciplined in the Kingdom." In the light of this fact, and the knowledge of the strenuous work involved, it is droll to study the lugubrious tone of his letters home—" six or seven campaigns, and an age in Scotland. I shall be sick of my office : the very bloom of life nipped in this northern climate," and again, " barren battalion conversation rather blunts the faculties than improves my youth and vigour bestowed idly in Scotland ; my temper daily charged with discontent ; and from a man become martinet or monster." Wolfe's sympathy and care for his men gives to the last words a humour that he did not intend.

To find an additional outlet for his energies he went back to his books, and engaged tutors to teach him Latin and mathematics. The college was apparently the only good thing he found in Glasgow, for he remarked " the men here are civil, designing and treacherous, with their immediate interests always in view ; they pursue trade with the warmth and necessary mercantile spirit, arising from the baseness of their other qualifications. The women, coarse, cold, and cunning, for ever enquiring after man's circumstances. They make that the standard of their good breeding." Elsewhere he says : " I do several things in my character of commanding officer which I should never think of

in any other : for instance, I'm every Sunday
at the Kirk, an example justly to be admired.
I would not lose two hours of a day if it did not
answer some end.　When I say ' lose two hours,'
I must explain to you that the generality of
Scotch preachers are excessive blockheads, so
truly and obstinately dull that they seem to
shut out knowledge at every entrance.　They
are not like our good folks.　Ours are priests,
and though friends to *venaison* they are friends
to sense."

Wolfe's views on Scotland were, beyond doubt,
prejudiced by the climate, which tried his health
severely.　For, as he confessed to his father,
" I'm sorry to say that my writings are greatly
influenced by the state of my body or mind at
the time of writing ; and I'm either happy or
ruined by my last night's rest, or from sunshine,
or light and sickly air ; such infirmity is the
mortal frame subject to."

A tall, lank, narrow-shouldered youth, the
lack of colour in his complexion emphasised by
the excess in his vivid red hair, he had not only
outgrown his strength but impaired it permanently through the undue strain to which
the undeveloped frame was forced by a too
ardent spirit.　This spirit had its visible expression in radiant blue eyes which transformed his
homely features, and in a firm mouth which

counteracted the receding chin, an inherited
characteristic. Wolfe seems ever conscious that
his life was a race between achievement and
disease, and, although he could forget his ills
in action, for that reason fretted over them
during the spells when opportunity tarried and
the goal seemed out of reach of his short span of
life. This tendency was perhaps increased by
having an ailing mother, whose correspondence
was filled with details of her own ills and the
even more ill remedies of Georgian quackery.

Wolfe's discontent, too, was augmented by the
barrenness of his efforts to lay siege to the heart
of Miss Lawson, a maid-of-honour to the Princess
of Wales. Although he saw her but little, and
gained no response, "absence made the heart
grow fonder," and the opposition of his parents,
who had their eyes on a "Croydon heiress with
£30,000," led to family discord when his mother
seemingly cast doubts on the honour of the maid-
of-honour's mother; and his blunter father
roundly castigated James Wolfe's "obstinacy and
perseverance in error." He makes a riposte
in a letter to his mother when he says sarcasti-
cally of the impending marriage of his maternal
aunt that it "is as pleasant a thing as I have
heard of a good while past. I suppose the man's
a philosopher, and has taken her to try how much
he can bear and what mankind with the assist-

ance of reason and learning is capable of suffer-
ing. I hope, as a grammarian, he does not
depend upon his rhetoric to keep her in good
humour."

Wolfe's cup of woe was filled to overflowing
when the Duke of Cumberland refused his
application to spend his leave at Metz studying
artillery and engineering. Some time before,
when his colonel, Lord George Sackville, had
advised him to spend his leave in London keeping up his "acquaintance amongst the heads
of our trade and procuring new ones that may
be of use," Wolfe had declared, "I have no turn
that way. If I'm really wanted, 'tis well to be
prepared." His idea of preparation was to
study foreign countries and armies, not the
drawing-rooms of London; and such was his
foresight, or second sight, that as early as 1749
he was writing to friends in America for details
of that theatre of war where lay his own future.
Wolfe's discontent was not due to selfish ambition, for his acting rank had been converted
into actual rank by his promotion to lieutenant-
colonel on the recommendation of Sackville and
with the approval of Cumberland. Few could
dream of such a rise when only twenty-three.
But he wished that his benefactors would take
wider views; and although he bowed to their
decision, he complained in various private letters

of the imbecility of those who " oppose the only
method that can be fallen upon to preserve any
knowledge of military affairs in the army."
" This is a dreadful mistake and, if obstinately
pursued, will disgust a number of good intentions,
and preserve that prevailing ignorance of military
affairs that has been so fatal to us in all our
undertakings . . . I am, nevertheless, still determined to employ some few years of my life
in the real business of a soldier, and not sacrifice
all my time to idling, as our trifling soldierships."
If Cumberland's refusal was due to a narrow-
ness of outlook, it was instigated by Lord Bury,
Sackville's successor as colonel of the regiment,
and in his case had the still less worthy motive
of selfishness—if Wolfe took long leave Bury
might have to tear himself away from the
pleasures of London to supervise the regiment.
For his visits were even less frequent than with
the majority of colonels in that period. Perhaps it was as well, for when ultimately he came
to see it at Inverness, his outrageous behaviour
marred the good feeling which Wolfe had striven
to create between the soldiers and the inhabitants.
The Corporation, essentially Jacobite, waited
upon him with an invitation to dinner, whereupon he insisted that it should be on the anni-
versary of Culloden, and forced them to agree
by the threat of a military riot.

With Wolfe the refusal of his leave abroad,
coming on top of his disappointment in love,
drove him to a brief plunge into dissipation
and the debauched follies which were then the
common fashion, but the first taste cured his
mind, if not his body.   For in manners as in
soldiering Wolfe was distinct from his times,
and one of his officers wrote, " our acting commander here is a paragon.   He neither drinks,
curses, gambles, nor runs after women.   So we
make him our pattern."

But Wolfe's letters show him too human to
become a prig : he can laugh at himself as a
juvenile commanding officer " that must do
justice to good and bad . . . one that must
study the tempers and dispositions of many men
in order to make their situation easy and agreeable to them . . . a mark set up for everybody
to observe and judge of ; and last of all, suppose
me employed in discouraging vice and recom-
mending the reverse at the turbulent age of
twenty-three, when it is possible I may have as
great a propensity that way as any of the men
that I converse with ! "   It is with a " blush "
that he confesses his own lack of vice, and
realises that " 'tis a disadvantage to be first
in an imperfect age ; either we become enamoured
of ourselves, seeing nothing superior, or fall into
the degree of our associates."   And he modestly

ascribes his own difference to the fact that " a
pretty constant employment helps to get me
through, and secures me from excess of debauch."

The regiment had moved from Glasgow to
Perth, where as a recreation he took to grouse-
shooting. The long days out on the moors,
" from five in the morning till night," benefited
him in health, if not in other ways, for he says :
" I, who am a very bad shot, had an equal
share of the labour, and less of the entertain-
ment." The country was now quiet, and the
presence of the troops compelled a state of law
and order hitherto unknown. " The Highlanders
are so narrowly watched that they are even
forced to abandon their favourite practice of
stealing cattle, and are either reduced to live
honestly and industriously, or starve through
excess of idleness." Wolfe had a strong vein of
humour, and tapped it frequently in Scotland.
Expressing his surprise that some Scottish officers
should have enjoyed their time at Gibraltar, he
remarks : " But it is not much to be wondered
at that they are contented in any part of the
world ; for I'm sure their native lot is fallen in
a barren ground." Again, when after a spell
at Banff the regiment moves to Inverness and
he seizes the chance to engage a tutor once more,
he writes to his father : " I have read the mathematics till I am grown perfectly stupid, and have

algebraically worked away the little portion of understanding that was allowed me."

An air of gravity is the way to the hearts of the local people. "And whoever goes to Kirk (as I do) once a week, and there comports himself with more reverence to the priest than consideration for the nature of the business—herein I sometimes fail,—will most assuredly deserve and obtain a reputation of great wisdom and discretion. We are allowed to be the most religious foot officers that have been in the North for many a day. . . . See the variety and constant change of things ; in most of our quarters we have been looked upon no better than as the sons of darkness, and given up unto Satan. Here we are white as the snow that covers the hills all about—not from want of temptation to sin, as you may believe, but from sudden conversion and power to resist."

But, in pursuit of his object of healing old sores, he tries a different route to the good favour of the women in the district—by giving dances every fortnight to " an assembly of female rebels, composed of Macdonalds, Frazers, and M'Intoshes. . . . They are perfectly wild as the hills that breed them ; but they lay aside their principles for the sake of sound and movement."

Perhaps it was the discovery of this panacea

for tranquillity, and his desire to develop it, that inspired him to renew his pleas for leave to go abroad on a visit to Paris. This was a desire, and a venue, that his superiors could understand and tolerate better than the study of artillery and engineering at Metz, and after some persistence he secured permission from the Commander-in-Chief. He made a detour by way of Ireland in order to visit his relatives there, particularly a soldier uncle with whom he had long kept up a correspondence on military affairs, interrupted occasionally when the older man took offence at his nephew's opinions as " an innovator in discipline." Arriving in Paris in October 1752, Wolfe adopted a way of life that would have surprised his seniors. " Four or five days a week I am up an hour before day (that is six hours sooner than any other fine gentleman in Paris). I ride, and as I told you in a former letter, I fence and dance, and have a master to teach me French. These occupations take up all the morning. I dine twice or three times at home "—in his lodgings—" sometimes at Lord Albemarle's "—the Ambassador —" and sometimes with my English acquaintances. After dinner I either go to the public entertainments or to visit, at nine I come home, and am in bed generally before eleven. . . . This way of living is directly opposite to the

practice of the place ; but I find it impossible
to pursue the business I came upon and to
comply with the customs and manners of the
inhabitants at the same time.   No constitu-
tion, however robust, could go through all."
His clear sense was not submerged by the glamour
of the Bourbon court, and its superficiality is
nowhere better exposed than in his epigrammatic
comment, " men that only desire to shine, and
that had rather say a smart thing than do a
great one. . . . A Frenchman that can make
his mistress laugh . . . is at the top of his
ambition."   Elsewhere he remarks : " The natives
in general are not handsome either in face or
figure ; but then they improve what they have."
His attitude was not governed by insular prejudice, for he could remark : " The people here
use umbrellas in hot weather to defend them
from the sun, and something of the same kind
to secure them from the sun and rain.   I wonder
that a practice so useful is not introduced
in England, where there are such frequent
showers. . . ."   He also benefited from the
attentions of a Paris dentist who filled his teeth
with lead, and suggests that his mother might
consult the dentist by post on the condition
of her gums and teeth.   An incidental note of
interest is that the post took five days from
London to Paris.   He was taken by the Ambas-

sador to Versailles, " a cold spectator of what
we commonly call splendour and magnificence.
A multitude of men and women were assembled
to bow and pay their compliments in the most
submissive manner to a creature of their own
species." Wolfe obviously had no taste for
flunkeyism, and even refused an offer of being
military tutor to the Duke of Richmond, excus-
ing himself to his somewhat irritated parents by
saying : " I can't take money from any one
but the King, my master. . . . The Duke of
Richmond's friendship will be an honour to
me, provided he turns out well, and serves his
country with reputation. . . . If he miscarries
from bad principles, I shall be the first to fly
from his intimacy."

Wolfe's own studies made good progress, if
more in fencing and riding than in dancing and
French. There are letters, however, from women
who danced with him on his return which suggest
that he was unduly modest of his own accomplishments—and mastery of the minuet was
more difficult than of the fox-trot. If the French
beauties left him cold, it was partly because the
image of Miss Lawson was fixed in his mind, for
he writes : " I never hear her name mentioned
without a twitch, or hardly ever think of her
with indifference." Not that he still cherished
hopes ; for in another letter he refers to a message

from "my friend Gage." "He says the little maid-of-honour is as amiable, and alas ! . . . as cold as ever. What can that lady mean by such obstinate self-denial ? or is she as much mistress of her own as of the hearts of all her acquaintances ? Is she the extraordinary woman that has no weakness ? or happily constructed without passions ? or lastly, and most likely, does she bid her reason choose ? She may push that matter too far, for common-sense demonstrates that one should not be a maid-of-honour too long . . . and there the matter *rests for ever*."

Disappointment did not urge Wolfe to seek consolation in amours, nor did it create an aversion to matrimony. When only twenty-four he had remarked that " men whose tenderness is not often called upon obtain by degrees— as you may particularly observe in old bachelors —a ferocity of nature, or insensibility about the misfortunes that befall others. There's no more tender-hearted person than a father or mother that has, or has had, many children." Frequently, too, he expresses his love for children, and in the way later he surrounds himself with dogs we may see an outlet for his thwarted desire. But, characteristically far - seeing, he realised other disadvantages in not marrying, epitomised in his comment : " Marshal Saxe

died in the arms of a little W . . . that plays
upon the Italian stage—an ignominious end for
a great conqueror."

After five months Wolfe tired of Paris, and
planned a visit to the French camps, but his
colonel had no patience with such a way of
spending leave, and promptly recalled him. Lord
Bury's excuse was that the major had suffered
a fit of apoplexy, and as he himself had no wish
to go to Scotland, Wolfe must. The journey
back in the new post-chaises—which so shook
him that he changed to post-horses, with almost
equal discomfort—was a prelude to the trials
which greeted him on his arrival. The major
dead, an ensign struck speechless with palsy,
another seized with convulsions the night of
his return, and the officers "impoverished, desperate, and without hopes of preferment." The
sorry welcome was at least a testimony to the
measure in which the wellbeing of the regiment
depended upon him. Another proof of the
patriarchal sway which this young man had
gained was the way in which the women of the
regiment wrote him while in Paris about their
troubles.

The regiment was back again in Glasgow,
and the circumstances of his return did not tend
to make him like it better on second acquaintance. He writes of "dinners and suppers of

the most execrable food upon earth, and wine that approaches to poison. The men drink till they are excessively drunk. The ladies are cold to everything but a bagpipe. I wrong them : there is not one that does not melt away at the sound of an estate ; there's the weak side of this soft sex."

But it would be wrong to take his letters too seriously. They were a safety vent for feelings constantly repressed in the interests of harmony and in his rôle of conciliator. There are many tributes to the good impression he had created among the people of the neighbourhood when in the autumn the regiment marched south, its tour of duty in Scotland at an end. And if he had done much to restore good relations, he was to be the means of forging still firmer links between Scotland and the British Army. As early as 1751, writing to his friend Rickson in America, he had suggested that Highland companies might be of use and well fitted for the colonial wars, and added, " How can you better employ a secret enemy than by making his end conducive to the common good ? " When war, the " Seven Years'," broke out in 1756, Pitt, then come into power, adopted a plan for raising two Highland battalions for service in America. This plan, which held out an offer of land grants as an attraction to recruits, was

delivered to Pitt, at Cumberland's suggestion, by
Lord Bury, who had then succeeded his father
as Earl of Albemarle, and as this absentee colonel
had never shown any desire to investigate
Highland conditions, it is a strong deduction
that he merely played the part of a post office
for Wolfe's ideas. And Wolfe was the first to
pay tribute to the Highlanders' fighting value
when he met them in America, adding that they
were " commanded by the most manly corps of
officers I ever saw."

On quitting Scotland the march south to the
regiment's new quarters at Dover was by way
of Carlisle, Warwick, and Reading, where his
passing left a memory of " a tall thin officer
astride a bay horse, his face lit up by a smile,
and conversing pleasantly with the officers who
rode by his side." His stay at Dover was short,
and next spring he was not sorry to leave this
bleak spot, with that " vile dungeon " its castle.
But the regiment's next station, Exeter, if
warmer in climate, had almost too warm a
political atmosphere—a hotbed of Jacobitism.
But he promptly applied his Inverness remedy
by giving regimental dances, and used harmonious sounds as a means to harmonious
relations. " Will you believe that no Devon-
shire squire dances more than I do ? What no
consideration of pleasure or complaisance for

the sex could effect, the love of peace and harmony has brought about. I have danced the
officers into the good graces of the Jacobite
women hereabouts, who were prejudiced against
them." If the means was subtle, the motive
was impeccable : "It is not our interest to
quarrel with any but the French ; and they
must be devilish minds that take a pleasure in
disputing."

The regiment had only been a few months in
Exeter when they were warned to be ready
to go on board the fleet at Bristol, presumably
for America or some other overseas expedition.
Wolfe's spirits rose at the thought of action,
and he refused to be damped even by his father's
pessimistic warnings about the rottenness of
amphibious campaigns—as he had experienced it
at Carthagena.

But the order tarried, and when it came was
instead for a change of station to Winchester.
On top of this disappointment another followed.
Lord Bury's succession to his father's title had
made vacant the colonelcy of the regiment.
Wolfe had cherished hopes of it, but the King
thought him "too young," and to increase his
mortification the officer ultimately appointed
had political rather than military claims. Wolfe
would not listen to a proposal that his father
might resign his own regimental command in

favour of him, refusing to jeopardise his parents'
income and security; but his discontent grew
as the chances of promotion and active service
alike seemed to be slipping away. The very
rapidity with which he had risen to lieutenant-
colonel at twenty-three made him impatient for
the next step. Like most men of genius he was
conscious of his own powers, neither depreciating
nor exaggerating them, and far from vain pride
had the common feeling of such men that his
superiority was due not to his own excellence
but to the deficiencies of other men. On this
point one of his letters is worth quoting at
length : " The officers of the army in general
are persons of so little application to business
and have been so ill educated that . . . a man
of common industry is in reputation amongst
them. I reckon it a very great misfortune to
this country that I . . . who have, I know,
but a very modest capacity, and some degree
of diligence little above the ordinary run, should
be thought, as I generally am, one of the best
officers of my rank in the service. I am not at
all vain of the distinction. The comparison
would do a man of genius very little honour,
and does not illustrate me by any means ; and
the consequence will be very fatal to me in
the end, for as I rise in rank people will expect
some considerable performances, and I shall be

induced, in support of an ill-got reputation, to be lavish of my life, and shall probably meet that fate which is the ordinary effect of such conduct." Here is true modesty, not the affectation which commonly masquerades for it. And how prophetic the final passage !

He was called from Winchester to Canterbury by an invasion scare, for war clouds had been gathering over that brief sea margin which separated the perpetual rivals, England and France, the atmosphere as tense and the watchers less deluded than in the years preceding 1914. Indeed, even while peace still held in name, spasmodic hostilities had begun.

In anticipation of a French landing, Wolfe issued orders to the regiment which shed light on his military ideas. Mobility is the keynote, and to this end the troops are to march light ; they are to carry out all exercises with their knapsacks on so that they may be accustomed to them and able to go into action direct from the march ; the attack is practised with the battalion delivering a " cool well-levelled " fire, while the Grenadiers and piquet sweep round and take the enemy in flank. And Wolfe warned them of his severe penalties if any took advantage of the confusion caused by an invasion to loot or pilfer from their own country-folk.

But when the war definitely came on 18th

May 1756, Wolfe's regiment marched not to resist invasion, nor to embark for a counter-blow, but to peaceful Devizes. A change in July to a special war camp pitched on Blandford Down looked more hopeful, for the assembly of six battalions of infantry, with cavalry and artillery, seemed to suggest the preparation of an expeditionary force. There was room for such preparation in Wolfe's views, for after a review and exercise of the troops, he wrote: "There are officers who had the presumption and vanity to applaud our operations, bad as they were; but I hope the General saw our defects and will apply a speedy remedy, without which I think we are in imminent danger of being cut to pieces in our first encounter." However, for a while no more strenuous test came than an excursion to Stroud to aid the civil power in dealing with riots among the Gloucestershire weavers. Wolfe succeeded in avoiding blood-shed, and just as in Paris he had interpreted the storm-signals of the coming revolution, so at Stroud his sympathetic insight led him to see the justice of the case of the "poor, half-starved weavers of broadcloth," and to restrain his men from action which might have fomented the bitterness. His wrath was kept for Byng and others in high places, who by their incompetency or neglect endangered the country he loved more than life. More than money too, for while he would not allow his parents to risk their security on behalf of his advancement, he urged his mother to persuade his father "to contribute all he can possibly afford towards the defence of the island—retrenching, if need be, his expenses, moderate as they are. I would have him engage in lotteries and all schemes of raising money, because I believe they are honestly intended; and though he should be considerably a loser the motive of his actions will overbalance his losses. Let the General keep a little ready money by him for his own use and yours, and with the rest, if he has it, assist the State; nay, I should go so far as to advise him to lend three or four thousand pounds to the Government without any interest at all, or give it, since it is the savings of his salaries and the reward of his services. Excuse this freedom." Yet for himself he was determined that his contribution should be in action, and if he could not make this directly under his country's colour he even thought of giving it indirectly by taking service in the army of England's ally, Frederick the Great of Prussia.

Whether this intention was more than a passing whim can never be known, for the long-awaited call rescued him, happily for England. He had been offered, by the Lord-Lieutenant, the post of Quartermaster-General in Ireland, and had reluctantly accepted partly to please his parents, and partly because it promised his colonelcy—which the King subsequently refused. At this juncture, when a year of half-hearted warfare had shaken our allies' confidence, Pitt was called to power, and changed inaction into direct action against the French coast— a blow at the naval arsenal at Rochefort, in the Bay of Biscay. Wolfe's regiment was one of those ordered to assemble in the Isle of Wight for the expedition, and he instantly seized the chance to relieve himself of his distasteful Irish appointment without offence to his patron.

Thus the turn of fortune's wheel brought him back seventeen years afterwards to the spot where, a lad of thirteen, he had hoped to begin his military career. If disillusionment had come in some directions his eagerness for battle was as great, and there was no regret for his choice. His philosophy and the military creed of the true soldier was never better expressed than in a letter written at Glasgow, wherein he said : " That variety incident to a military life gives our profession some advantage over those of a more even and consistent nature. We have all our passions and affections roused and exercised, many of which must have wanted their proper employment, had not suitable occasions obliged us to exert them.   Few men are acquainted with the degree of their own courage till danger prove them, and are seldom justly informed how far the love of honour and the dread of shame are superior to the love of life. . . . Constancy of temper, patience, and all the virtues necessary to make us suffer with a good grace are likewise parts of our character, and . . . frequently called in to carry us through unusual difficulties.   What moderation and humility must he be possessed of that bears the good fortune of a successful war with tolerable modesty and humility, and he is very excellent in his nature who triumphs without insolence.   A battle gained is, I believe, the highest joy mankind is capable of receiving to him who commands ; and his merit must be equal to his success if it works no change to his disadvantage.   Lastly, a defeat is a trial of human resolution, and to labour under the mortification of being surpassed, and to live to see the fatal consequences that may follow to one's country, is a situation next to damnable."

His " brightest joy " was conceived of as the fire in which character was tried and purified. He was no swashbuckler, loving fighting for fighting's sake, living only for the moment. But like the knight of old, chivalry's ideal if not its common reality, he had by exercise and

silent meditation prepared himself for the trial
to which his life was dedicated.   Five years
before, he had written: "The winters wear
away, so do our years, and so does life itself;
and it matters little where a man passes his days
and what station he fills, or whether he be
great or considerable, but it imports him something to look to his manner of life.   This day
I am twenty-five years of age, and all that time
is as nothing. . . . But it is worth a moment's
consideration that one may be called away on
a sudden, unguarded and unprepared;   and
the oftener these thoughts are entertained the
less will be the dread or fear of death.   You
will judge by this sort of discourse that it is
the dead of night, when all is quiet and at rest,
and one of those intervals when men think of
what they really are, and what they really
should be;   how much is expected and how
little performed. . . . The little time taken
for meditation is the best employed in all our
lives;   for, if the uncertainty of our state and
being is then brought before us, and that compared with our course of conduct, who is there
that won't immediately discover the inconsis-
tency of all his behaviour and the vanity of all
his pursuits?"   And from this meditation came
the resolve, in humility put on the lowliest
plane: "Better be a savage of some use than

a gentle amorous puppy, obnoxious to all the world."

This spiritual preparation was but the accompaniment of a mental and material preparation in which he was an equally stern taskmaster to himself. In fitting himself for his future rôle he foreshadowed Napoleon's maxim "read and reread," and his enthusiasm for study infected others, until there gathered round him a band of young disciples to whom he acted as guide in the paths of knowledge. One such letter is worth quoting from, because it sheds light not merely on the breadth of Wolfe's reading but on the military classics of his age. It is addressed to Thomas Townshend, the future Lord Sydney, whose younger brother was anxious to qualify himself for a career in which he later won distinction—"As to the books that are fittest for this purpose he may begin with the 'King of Prussia's Regulations for his Horse and Foot,' where the economy and good order of an army in the lower branches are extremely well established. Then there are the 'Memoirs' of the Marquis de Santa Cruz, Feuquières, and Montecuculi; Folard's 'Commentaries upon Polybius'; the 'Projet de Tactique'; 'L'Attaque et la Défense des Places,' par le Maréchal de Vauban; 'Les Memoires de Goulon'; 'L'Ingenieur de Cam-

pagne.' Le Sieur Renie for all that concerns
artillery. Of the ancients Vegetius, Cæsar, Thu-
cydides, Xenophon's ' Life of Cyrus ' and ' Retreat of the Ten Thousand Greeks.' I do not
mention Polybius, because the Commentaries
and the History naturally go together. Of
latter days Davila, Guicciardini, Strada, and
the ' Memoirs of the Duc de Sully.' There is
an abundance of military knowledge to be picked
out of the lives of Gustavus Adolphus and
Charles XII., King of Sweden, and of Zisca
the Bohemian ; and if a tolerable account
could be got of the exploits of Scanderbeg it
would be inestimable, for he excels all the
officers, ancient and modern, in the conduct
of a small defensive army. . . . The ' Life of
Suetonius,' too, contains many fine things in
this way . . . and there is a little volume
entitled ' Traité de la Petite Guerre ' that your
brother should take in his pocket when he goes
on out-duty and detachments. The Maréchal
de Puységur's book, too, is in esteem. . . . It
is much to be wished that all our young soldiers
of birth and education would follow your
brother's steps, and, as they will have their
turn to command, that they would try to make
themselves fit for the important trust ; without it
we must sink under the superior abilities and indefatigable industry of our restless neighbours."

It is noteworthy that Wolfe drew inspiration from Xenophon's ' Cyropædia,' the fountain-head of military thought, as had two of the greatest captains, Gustavus and Scipio—who carried this book on all his campaigns. And in Wolfe's prefacing remarks we find the key to his zeal for mathematics while in Scotland—" Your brother, no doubt, is master of the Latin and French languages, and has some knowledge of the mathematics ; without the last he can never become acquainted with one considerable branch of our business, the construction of fortifications and the attack and defence of places. . . ." Nor was his reading exclusively utilitarian, as is shown by references elsewhere to such books as Montesquieu's ' L'Esprit des Lois,' not less than by his recital of Gray's ' Elegy ' at the most critical hour of his life.

If his material preparation was devoted to his own regiment, with results which we have already quoted, he preceded Frederick, as he foreshadowed Wellington, in his recognition of the decisiveness of fire-power and its superiority over shock-action. And no man ever better proved the truth of his theories than Wolfe at Quebec, where one perfect volley won not only a battle but an empire. Wolfe might well be called the father of modern musketry training. In Scotland he developed a scheme of constant ball practice at varied targets— " firing balls at objects teaches the soldier to level incomparably, makes the recruits steady, and removes the foolish apprehension that seizes young soldiers when they first load their arms with bullets. We fire, first singly, then by files 1, 2, 3, or more, then by ranks, and lastly by platoons ; and the soldiers see the effects of their shot, especially at a mark or upon water. We shoot obliquely, and in different situations of ground, from heights, downwards, and contrarywise."

Like most constructive reformers he was fiercely critical of obstruction and incompetence. " We are lazy in time of peace, and, of course, want vigilance and activity in war. Our military education is by far the worst in Europe. We are the most egregious blunderers in war that ever took the hatchet in hand." " I'm tired of proposing anything to the officers that command our regiments ; they are in general so lazy and so bigoted to old habits." When in Canterbury he heard that his old commander of the " '45 " was coming to take over command of the garrison, and it moved him to write : " General Hawley is expected in a few days to keep us all in order ; if there is an invasion they could not make use of a more unfit person.

The troops dread his severity, hate the man, and hold his military knowledge in contempt."

Wolfe might have fared badly under the present-day rules for promotion by selection, rules which despite their general soundness may lend themselves to abuse by the well-meant clause which reduces the fine word " loyalty " to the narrower sense and requirement of " loyalty to superiors." Yet by the irony of history he is to-day a tradition and a model held up for the young, who if they presumed to imitate either his original or his critical outlook, might be castigated as impertinent and their prospects damned. Wolfe's reasons and justification are well put in a letter after revisiting the battlefield of Culloden, when he found " room for a military criticism as well as a place for a little ridicule upon some famous transactions of that memorable day. . . . But why this censure when the affair is so happily decided ? To exercise one's ill-nature ? No, to exercise the faculty of judging. . . . The more a soldier thinks of the false steps of those that are gone before, the more likely he is to avoid them." Wolfe recognised a higher loyalty than that to superiors—to the weal of the army and the nation. In action no more faithful subordinate, in reflection none more critical. For that " la critique est la vie de la science " is a greater truth than the idea, prevalent among weak superiors, that it is a breach of discipline.

If the British Army of Wolfe's day was so bad as it is painted, it is to its credit that such a habit of outspoken criticism did not prevent his rapid rise, and that his superiors could see beyond this to the solid work upon which it was supported. Thus the years of personal preparation and national peace, so long to Wolfe, so short in reality, brought him his chance in the Rochefort expedition. Seventeen years of preparation were to be followed by two brief years of fulfilment. In this expedition "nothing was wanting to ensure success but a general," but owing to this want the armada returned home with nothing accomplished, at the cost of less than ten men but a million of money. Wolfe's own forecast in a letter to his friend Major Rickson, recipient of many confidences, was not promising: "I can't flatter you with a lively picture of my hopes as to the success of it; the reasons are so strong against us in whatever we take in hand that I never expect any great matter; the chiefs, the engineers, and our wretched discipline are the great and insurmountable obstructions." The chiefs were Sir John Mordaunt, Conway, and Cornwallis for the army, while Admiral Hawke commanded the fleet. Instead of striking swiftly, they

dallied in sight of the French coast, giving the
enemy warning to strengthen his defences, and
failed to make up their minds to a definite course
of action.   The fleet arrived off the Île de Ré
on 20th September 1757, and on 23rd September
Captain Howe subdued the fortress on Île d'Aix
by a single-handed effort.

Meanwhile Wolfe presumed on his friendship
with Mordaunt to obtain permission to go ashore
to reconnoitre directly the fortress surrendered.
Lying off in a boat, he landed immediately,
and, climbing one of the works, studied the
mainland through a telescope.   On his return
he gave his opinion that after a fort on the pro-
montory of Fouras had been destroyed, as a
necessary first step, a landing could well be made
on the beach of Châtelaillon, a little to the north
between Rochefort and La Rochelle.   After
interminable discussions and councils of war, the
troops embarked in boats on the night of 28th
September ;   and, after waiting several hours,
were ordered to return to the fleet.   Hawke
thereupon lost patience with the generals, and
they in turn yielded to his insistence for a return
to England.

While many reputations were blasted, Wolfe
emerged with public honour, for the Court of
Inquiry in their report declared that his plan,
if carried out, " certainly must have been of the

greatest utility towards carrying your Majesty's instructions into execution." Before the inquiry began, Wolfe's merit had been recognised by his promotion to brevet-colonel, and early in 1758 he was appointed colonel of the newly raised 67th Foot (now the 2nd Battalion the Hampshire Regiment).

But best of all, his experience led him to formulate the principles which should govern amphibious operations in a letter to Major Rickson, which the late Sir Julian Corbett has termed " a priceless document," and one " that every commander to whom such operations are committed might do worse than lay under his pillow."

" I have found out that an Admiral should endeavour to run into an enemy's port immediately after he appears before it ; that he should anchor the transport ships and frigates as close as he can to the land ; that he should reconnoitre and observe it as quick as possible, and lose no time in getting the troops on shore ; that previous directions should be given in respect to landing troops, and a proper disposition made for boats of all sorts, appointing leaders and fit persons for conducting the different divisions. On the other hand, experience shows me that, in an affair depending on vigour and despatch, the generals should settle their plan of operations, so that no time may be lost in idle debate and consultations when the sword should be drawn ; that pushing on smartly is the road to success, and more particularly so in an affair of this sort ; that nothing is to be reckoned an obstacle to your undertaking which is not found really so on trial ; that in war something must be allowed to chance and fortune, seeing that it is in its nature hazardous, and an option of difficulties ; that the greatness of an object should come under consideration, opposed to the impediments that lie in the way ; that the honour of one's country is to have some weight ; and that, in particular circumstances and times, the loss of a thousand men is rather an advantage to a nation than otherwise, seeing that gallant attempts raise its reputation . . . whereas the contrary appearances sink the credit of a country, ruin the troops, and create infinite uneasiness and discontent at home."

Baulked at Rochefort, Pitt now turned his gaze westwards. " In America, England and France were to be fought for," he declared. And for once England had a minister strong enough to sweep aside military custom and seniority, and, " passing over whole columns of the army list," to pick his own instruments.

The main expedition was to be against the great French fortress of Louisburg, on Cape

Breton Island, which dominated the sea approaches to Canada. Louisburg, the Port Arthur of " Far Western " France, had been captured once before, in 1745, when weakly garrisoned, but restored by the peace treaty of 1748. It was a sorry reward for the gallant New England force which, without professional support, save for an English naval squadron, had forced this outer gate of Canada ; and, as with Heligoland, England had cause to regret the light-hearted way in which she had ceded it.

Pitt chose Colonel Jeffrey Amherst to command the expedition, creating him a major-general, and Wolfe was to go as one of his brigadiers. A miserable sailor, Wolfe suffered badly during the voyage, but fought down his sea-sickness, as he always did his more deep-seated maladies, when action was imminent.

After reconnoitring the rocky and forbidding coast-line in a sloop with Amherst, the plan was decided upon that Wolfe should make the real landing at Freshwater Cove in Gabarus Bay, some two miles west of Louisburg, while the other two brigadiers feinted to land at points nearer the fortress. This was different from Wolfe's own plan devised while waiting at Halifax for Amherst's arrival. His idea had been to land at three points north and east of Louisburg for a converging march on the fortress, while the fleet with a small detachment of troops threatened Gabarus Bay. This plan savours rather of Wolfe's much criticised dispersion of his forces later at Quebec, but he hoped thereby to confuse the defence and thereby ensure a landing. Moreover, he knew that the enemy had strongly entrenched the shore of Gabarus Bay, the obvious landing-place.

As it was, Wolfe had to make his landing— 8th June 1758—at the most strongly defended point, and the boats were greeted with such a hail of shot that Wolfe had to signal to them to sheer off. Three, however, on the extreme right were partially sheltered by a projecting spit of land, and touched bottom among the rocks at this point. Wolfe immediately directed the rest of the boats towards this landing ; and although many were stove in, the bulk of the troops scrambled ashore, led by Wolfe, who carried a cane as his only weapon. They pressed forward, and took the nearest French battery in flank by assault. Meanwhile another brigade, taking advantage of the enemy's attention being occupied by Wolfe, landed farther west. The French, thus menaced on both flanks, fled before their retreat to Louisburg was cut, leaving their guns in the hands of the British. But the next steps were more prolonged, and the delay thus caused impaired the greater plan for the con-

quest of Canada, preventing the release of
Amherst's force for co-operation with Abercrombie in the campaign on the mainland.
Louisburg harbour was a C shape, with the
fortified town at the lower extremity and
the mile-wide entrance narrowed to less than
half that distance by a chain of rocky islets
from Louisburg northwards, ending in Goat
Island.

Wolfe realised that if the battery on this island
could be subdued, its fall would open a way for
the fleet, and, with Amherst's approval, marched
round the harbour and seized Lighthouse Point
at the upper extremity. Erecting a battery
here, by strenuous efforts, he silenced the Goat
Island battery by 25th June ; but Admiral
Boscawen was slow to take advantage of the
opening, and four nights later the French blocked
the entrance anew by sinking ships. Wolfe
then returned to join in the direct overland
attack, and by alternate " shouldering " advances
on either flank worked ever closer to the fortress,
while his light infantry by constant skirmishing
wore down the enemy's resistance. One of his
officers is said to have remarked that their
harassing tactics, striking and then quickly falling back to shelter, reminded him of Xenophon's
account of the Καρδουχοι, to which Wolfe replied : " I had it from Xenophon, but our

friends here are astonished at what I have done because they have read nothing."

But the decisive factor came from the heavy battery which he had got into position on the hills overlooking Louisburg harbour from the north-west, and on 27th July the French capitulated. When this bombardment began they had made complaints that civilians were being killed, and Wolfe in passing them on remarked : " When the French are in a scrape they are ready to cry out on behalf of the human species ; when fortune favours them, none more bloody, more inhuman."

Seven weeks after the landing the strongest fortress in the New World had fallen, but Wolfe was dissatisfied. His letters are characteristic : " We made a rash and ill-advised attempt to land, and by the greatest of good fortune imaginable we succeeded. If we had known the country and had acted with more vigour, half the garrison at least (for they were all out) must have fallen into our hands immediately we landed. Our next operations were exceedingly slow and injudicious. . . ." As he had criticised the delay at Halifax, the failure to provide fresh meat, and equipment suitable for a colonial campaign, so now he wrote : " I cannot penetrate the General's intentions. If he means to attack Quebec he must not lose a moment." But while

many officers suffered from his scathing pen, he
gave generous praise to an old personal enemy,
Murray, and a strong private recommendation
for his promotion.

Again, Wolfe had no use for the American
colonial troops, " the dirtiest most contemptible
cowardly dogs that you can conceive " ; but in
an inspired passage he prophesies that, despite
present drawbacks, " this will, some time hence,
be a vast empire, the seat of power and learning.
Nature has refused them nothing, and there will
grow a people out of our little spot, England,
that will fill this vast space, and divide this
great portion of the globe with the Spaniards,
who are possessed of the other half."

As the naval authorities were reluctant to
chance the risks of the passage up the river St
Lawrence, Wolfe departed to harry the French
settlements on the Gulf of St Lawrence as a
diversion to occupy the attention of Montcalm,
the French commander in Canada, and prevent
him reinforcing the troops who were opposing
Abercrombie's overland advance. Before Wolfe
returned to Louisburg, Amherst had sailed for
New York to support Abercrombie. A letter
which Wolfe sent after him gives a sidelight on
the influence that Wolfe had won, allowing him
to give advice to his superior : " An offensive
daring kind of war will save the Indians and

ruin the French.   Blockhouses, and a trembling
defensive, encourage the meanest scoundrels to
attack us.   The navy showed their happy disposition for plundering upon this, as on former
occasions, and I indulged them to the utmost.
I wish you success.   Cannonade furiously before
you attack, and don't let them go on in lines,
but rather in columns."   And giving a rough
diagram of the two formations, after that of
the line, he adds : " Cela ne vaut rien pour les
retranchements."   The first part of this advice
gives a clue to the motive of Wolfe's strategy
at Quebec the following year.   The second part
epitomises the principles of a trench warfare
attack.   It was a pity that our leaders in the
early years of the last war had not read, or
digested, Wolfe's letters.   The column to break
through a deep system of defence ; the line in
open warfare to deliver the greatest possible
concentration of fire in the shortest possible
time.

Wolfe then sailed for England to recover his
health, which had suffered from the strain.   Pitt
had intended him to remain in America, but
the order had missed him, and hearing this,
Wolfe wrote to put himself right with the minister,
expressing his willingness to serve again " in
America, and particularly in the river St Lawrence."   Pitt had learnt from many sources to

whom was due the chief credit of the Louisburg victory, and Wolfe's letter gave him the assurance upon which to take the momentous decision of giving this young soldier of thirty-two the command of the expedition now planned against Quebec. Wolfe was then recuperating at Bath, as well as beginning his second brief love affair —with Miss Katherine Lowther, whom he had met on a brief visit to Bath just before sailing for Louisburg. Miss Lowther yielded to his siege as completely as Louisburg, but this successful courtship was destined to be as short as his first unsuccessful courtship had been long. On receiving Pitt's summons, Wolfe hastened to London, and the two remaining months before he sailed were occupied with preparations. Pitt's prestige had enabled him to override seniority in choosing his commanders, and Wolfe in turn was able to choose his own subordinates. He named Monckton and Murray, the old enemy who had won his praise at Louisburg, as two of his brigadiers, and accepted Pitt's suggestion of Townshend as the third. Moreover, he was even able to overcome the King's obstinate objection to Colonel Carleton and secure him as Quartermaster - General. The conservative George II. was so far converted by Wolfe's merit and the disasters which had befallen earlier commanders, that when Newcastle declared that Wolfe was mad, he retorted : " Mad, is he ? Then all I can say is, I hope he'll bite some of my other generals." But crusted seniority scored in the last round by ensuring that this upstart youth was only given the local rank of major-general while in America. And although Pitt had intended him to have 12,000 men, Wolfe found less than 9000 available at Louisburg, his base, and many deficiencies in equipment ; while Amherst's joint overland advance from New York was so tardy that the French were able to concentrate some 16,000 men round Quebec to oppose Wolfe. Luckily their quality was low, and their great commander, Montcalm, repeatedly thwarted by the Governor and his corrupt subordinates, but even so they had a position deemed impregnable. Quebec itself was perched loftily on the north shore of the St Lawrence, its guns commanding the river, while the land approach was barred by the rivers Montmorency and St Charles, and above Quebec by the cliffs of the plateau since famous as the Heights of Abraham. Observers have remarked a strange similarity between these forbidding cliffs and those which barred, likewise in vain, the landing at Anzac a century and a half later.

Trusting in this obstacle and in the guns of the city to control the narrow passage which led to the upper reaches of the river, Montcalm entrenched his army on the north shore just below Quebec, between the St Charles and the Montmorency.

Wolfe sailed from England in the middle of February after a farewell to his parents which in its Spartan brevity shatters various imaginative accounts which have survived—by a letter in which he said : " The formality of taking leave should be as far as possible avoided ; therefore I prefer this method of offering my good wishes and duty to my father and you. I shall carry this business through with my best abilities. The rest, you know, is in the hands of Providence, to whose care I hope your good life and conduct will recommend your son."

On reaching the American side he found to his disgust that Rear-Admiral Durell was still at anchor at Halifax—30th April,—having thus failed to carry out Wolfe's instructions to block the entrance to the St Lawrence directly the ice began to melt. As a result of this delay, although Durell was sent off at once, three French frigates and a score of storeships slipped through and up to Quebec before the entrance was closed, strengthening Montcalm's position and injuring Wolfe's plan. Fortunately Vice-Admiral Saunders, who had command of the main fleet, which had sailed with Wolfe from

England, was a man of different stamp, a fit
coadjutor for the army commander, and their
co-operation was to provide perhaps the finest
example in our history of combined action between
navy and army.   More delay, however, was
caused because Louisburg harbour was still
blocked with ice.   But although Wolfe could only
land there in the middle of May, he completed
his preparations and sailed by 1st June.   It is
worth note that he had insisted on a high proportion of light infantry, and had practised them
in a new exercise.

The voyage to Quebec was not the least
hazardous phase of the expedition, for the
currents and shoals of the St Lawrence were
notorious, and its achievement—due largely to
the skill of Captain Cook, later famous as the
discoverer—astonished the French.   Vaudreuil,
the governor, wrote : " The enemy have passed
sixty ships of war where we dare not risk a
vessel of a hundred tons by night and day."
Wolfe disembarked on the Isle of Orleans, four
miles below Quebec, on 27th June.   His reconnaissance revealed the French dispositions and
the way Durell's negligence had enabled them
to prepare to meet the attack.   A further taste
followed, for on the next day they loosed seven
fireships, but the coolness of the British seamen,
who rowed out and towed them ashore, averted

the danger. Wolfe retorted by a prompt stroke, seizing Point Lévis on the south bank of the river opposite Quebec, whence his guns could bombard the city. With an enemy strongly entrenched in a position which commanded the approach to Quebec, Wolfe's problem was to lure him out of his fastness. The only way of doing this was to bait the trap, and to this end Wolfe, who had already despatched Monckton's brigade to Point Lévis, now landed (8th July) the bulk of Townshend's and Murray's brigades on the north shore, just below the Montmorency River. This dispersion of his force has been much criticised, even by Fortescue ; but the objections, while in consonance with abstract theory, seem to overlook the actual circumstances. One is reminded of Foch's favourite anecdote about Verdy du Vernois at the battle of Nachod. Wracking his memory in vain to find a precedent or military axiom which might guide him in the difficult situation with which he was confronted, Verdy du Vernois exclaimed : " To the devil with history and principles ! After all, what is the problem ? "

The first essential in forming or judging any plan is to be clear as to the commander's true object, and the second to know the conditions. Knowing Wolfe's object and the almost impregnable position in which Montcalm was posted, had he any alternative but to take risks in order if possible to provide a bait which would lure the enemy from his entrenchments into the open ?   And I suggest that the risks were slight. Wolfe's command of the river gave him the power of movement, for reinforcement of either portion if engaged.   His distribution gave him the power of surprise, by keeping Montcalm in uncertainty and apprehension as to the direction of Wolfe's real move.   He had ample evidence that the French were disinclined to take the offensive, and his confidence in the strong superiority of his own troops in any engagement on their own ground—a confidence which was abundantly justified—gave him security that any part that was attacked could hold its own for the time until reinforcements crossed the river.

This understanding of Wolfe's object and the conditions sheds light on Townshend's statement, and complaint, that on inspecting his front Wolfe " disapproved of it, saying I had indeed made myself secure, for I had made a fortress." Townshend failed to realise that he was spoiling Wolfe's bait, for if the French would not come out to attack the English in the open, they certainly would not venture against them when visibly in a strongly fortified position.

So far from Wolfe being in danger, neither this bait nor the gradual destruction of the city by bombardment could stir the resolute and wary French commander. The next move was a naval one. On the night of 18th July a frigate and some smaller vessels slipped past the guns of Quebec under cover of a heavy British bombardment from Point Lévis, and anchored above the city. This at least forced Montcalm to detach 600 men to guard the few paths up the cliffs in the eight-mile stretch between Quebec and Cap Rouge. Wolfe at once reconnoitred the upper river for a possible landing on the north shore, but after restless meditation decided that both the difficulties and the risks were too great. As he wrote to Pitt: "What I feared most was, that if we should have landed between the town and the river of Cap Rouge, the body first landed could not be reinforced before they were attacked by the enemy's whole army." To land still higher up the river, as some critics have suggested, would not only have given Montcalm time to occupy fresh lines on that side, but have widely separated Wolfe's army from the main part of the fleet and his base—a far more dangerous dispersion than that which these critics condemn at Point Lévis and Montmorency. His communications would have been stretched like a narrow cord with a knife—Quebec—grazing the middle.

But the weeks were slipping by, and Wolfe

felt bound to try some daring measure to draw out the French, if he could find one less desperate than a landing above Quebec. Below Quebec he was separated from the French by the Montmorency, flowing swift and deep for many miles until it tumbled over the Falls, a two hundred and fifty feet drop, just before entering the St Lawrence. He had tried in vain to discover a practicable ford by which he could turn the gorge-protected front of the French, but below the Falls the river ran broad and shallow and could be waded near its mouth. A mile to the west, up the St Lawrence, there was a narrow strip of land between the river and the heights where the French had built redoubts. Wolfe now planned to land here with all the available grenadiers and part of Monckton's brigade from Point Lévis, hoping, by the capture of a detached redoubt, to tempt the French army down to regain it, and so bring on a battle in the open. Meanwhile the other two brigades were to be ready to ford the lower reaches of the Montmorency and join him.

On 31st July the attempt was made, covered by the guns of several ships and by the batteries across the Montmorency gorge. But on nearing the shore Wolfe perceived that the redoubt was "too much commanded to be kept without very great loss," and drew off. For several hours

the boats rowed up and down-stream, both to
confuse the enemy and to enable Wolfe to sight
another landing point.   Late in the afternoon
the enemy, marching and counter - marching,
seemed in some confusion, and Wolfe gave the
signal for a fresh attempt.   Unluckily many of
the boats grounded on an unseen ledge, causing
further delay.   Worse was to follow, for when
the troops got ashore, the grenadiers rushed
impetuously on the enemy's entrenchments without waiting for the main body to form up.   As
a storm of fire broke in their faces, a storm of
rain broke on their heads, and the steep slopes,
slippery with blood and rain, became unclimb-
able, as the muskets became unfireable.   Realising that his plans had gone awry, Wolfe broke
off the fight and re-embarked the troops.   It
was a severe set-back, and the French were
proportionately elated.   The Governor wrote,
" I have no more anxiety about Quebec."

Although neither in his frank despatches to
Pitt nor to his troops did Wolfe show any loss
of heart, a last letter to his mother reveals his
despair, and that he felt himself a ruined man.
For he knew that where age can blunder and
be forgiven, youth must seal its presumption
with success if it is to survive inevitable jealousy.
Dejected in mind, he fell ill in body, but saying,
" I know perfectly well you cannot cure my

complaint," demanded of his surgeon, " Patch me up so that I may be able to do my duty for the next few days, and I shall be content." He had been laid low on 19th August, but before this he had initiated a " starvation " campaign against the French, sending detachments to lay waste the country round, although he gave strict orders for the good treatment of women and children.   More important still was a move to cut off their main supplies which came down-stream from Montreal.   For weeks past, more and more ships had slipped past the guns of Quebec, and on 5th August, after being joined by Murray with 1200 troops in flat boats, they were sent up-stream to harass the French shipping and shores.   The diversion, moreover, forced Montcalm to detach another 1500 men under Bougainville to prevent a landing.   Economic pressure, however, is a slow weapon, and Wolfe feared that winter might stop operations before it could achieve its object.   From his sick-bed he sent a message asking his brigadiers to consult together on a fresh move, suggesting three possible variations of the Montmorency plan.   Murray had now returned, and the three, in reply, pro-posed instead " to carry the operations above the town," and try " to establish ourselves on the north shore," but without any detailed suggestions as to how and where it was to be done. Wolfe, as we know, had conceived this idea before, and reluctantly abandoned it, but now the situation was modified, both because he had got so many of his ships up river, and because, after the Montmorency plan had failed, a gamble was more justified and inevitable.

On 3rd September Wolfe evacuated the Montmorency camp, and on the 5th, after concentrating his forces on the south shore, marched the bulk, some 3600, overland up the river bank, and embarked them in the ships. Montcalm thereupon reinforced Bougainville, who was at the Cap Rouge, with another 1500 men, although feeling confident that it was a ruse of Wolfe's, who " is just the man to double back in the night."

Each day the ships drifted up and down with the tide, perplexing the French command and wearing out their troops with ceaseless marching and counter-marching, while Wolfe reconnoitred the cliffs through a telescope for a possible point of ascent. While his brigadiers were searching elsewhere, he observed a winding path up the cliffs at the Anse du Foulon, only a mile and a half above Quebec, and noticed that it was capped by a cluster of less than a dozen tents. Deeming the spot almost inaccessible, the French had posted there only a small piquet.

Wolfe's choice was made, but he kept it secret

until the eve of the venture. On the 10th he
informed Colonel Burton, of the 48th Regiment,
who was to be left in charge of the troops on the
south shore, and on the 11th he issued a warning
order for the embarkation of the troops next
night. On the 12th he issued his orders for
the attack, ending on the note, " The officers
and men will remember what their country
expects of them . . . resolute in the execution
of their duty "—the germ of Nelson's message
at Trafalgar. That evening, in his cabin on
H.M.S. *Sutherland*, he sent for his old school-
fellow of Greenwich, John Jervis—later famous
as Lord St Vincent, and now commanding a
sloop,—and gave him his will and a portrait
of Miss Lowther to be returned to her in the
event of his death.

Just before sunset Admiral Saunders with
the main fleet drew out along the shore opposite
Montcalm's camp below Quebec, and, lowering
their boats to suggest a landing, opened a violent
fire. This ruse admirably fulfilled its purpose
of fixing the enemy, for Montcalm concentrated
his troops and kept them under arms during
the night—miles away from the real danger
point. And while they were straining their
eyes to detect the threatened landing, a single
lantern rose to the maintop of the *Sutherland*,
miles up river, and 1600 troops of the first

division noiselessly embarked in their flat-boats. At 2 A.M. as the tide began to ebb, two lanterns rose and flickered, and the whole flotilla dropped silently down-stream, the troops in boats leading. Discovery was narrowly averted when a French-speaking officer twice replied to a sentry's challenge from the shore, his deception helped by the fact, of which two deserters had informed Wolfe, that the enemy were expecting a convoy of provisions.

At this crisis of his life, Wolfe, as all know who know nought else of Wolfe, was reciting the lines of Gray's elegy—" The paths of glory lead but to the grave "—and saying to those near him, " I would sooner have written that poem than take Quebec."

The landing was safely made at the Foulon cove : a band of picked volunteers swarmed up the steep face of the cliff, and, overpowering the French piquet on the summit, covered the landing of the main body. Before dawn the army, reinforced by another 1200 troops under Colonel Burton direct from the south bank, were moving towards Quebec. Wolfe had found, on the Heights of Abraham, the open battlefield for which he had thirsted. Should he be beaten he was certainly in a desperate position, but he had sure ground for confidence in the quality of his own men to offset the French quantity in open battle. There was a danger that Bougainville might hasten back from Cap Rouge and fall on his rear, but this menace can easily be exaggerated, and the light infantry which Wolfe detached to guard his rear was capable of holding Bougainville in check. A worse danger was that Montcalm might still decline battle, in which case the difficulty of bringing up supplies and artillery might make Wolfe's position precarious. But a military appreciation must consider the moral as well as the material elements, and Wolfe's appearance on the Heights of Abraham was a moral challenge that an enemy could hardly decline.

Wolfe disposed his force in a single line—to gain the utmost fire effect, wherein lay his strength,—with his left thrown back to guard the inland flank, and one regiment—Webb's (the 48th)—in reserve. Montcalm, warned too late, hurried his troops westwards across the St Charles and through the city. Wolfe's bait this time had succeeded, even beyond expectation, and Montcalm attacked before his whole force was on the spot, probably because the other part were pinned by fear of the threatened landing below Quebec.

The clash was preceded by an attempt of the Canadian irregulars and Indians to work round Wolfe's left, but if their fire was galling, their

effort was too uncontrolled to be effective.
About 10 A.M. the French main body advanced,
but their ragged fire drew no reply from the
British line, obedient to Wolfe's instructions
that " a cool well-levelled fire is much more
destructive and formidable than the quickest
fire in confusion." He himself was shot through
the wrist, but, wrapping a handkerchief round
it, continued his calls to the men to hold their
fire.   At last, when the French were barely
forty yards distant, the word was given, and
the British line delivered a shattering volley,
repeated it, and then, on Wolfe's signal, charged
a foe already disintegrating. At the head of
his picked grenadiers Wolfe was an inevitable
target.   A bullet penetrated his groin, a second
his lungs, and he fell, unobserved by the charging
ranks.   Only an officer and two others, soon
joined by an artillery officer, saw what happened, and began to carry him to the rear.
But realising that the wound was mortal, he
bade them put him down, and stopped them
sending for a surgeon. A few minutes later his
spirit had passed.   His dying words, when told
that the enemy were on the run—" Now God
be praised, I die happy,"—are historic.   But
the words immediately preceding these are a
finer tribute to him as a general—even on the
point of death : " Go, one of you, with all speed

to Colonel Burton and tell him to march Webb's regiment down to the St Charles River, and cut off the retreat of the fugitives to the bridge."

Monckton, too, had fallen wounded, and the command thus passed to Townshend, who checked the pursuit—which might have rushed the city gates on the heels of the flying foe—in order to reform the army and turn about to face Bougain-ville's belated approach. The sight of the British, emphasised by a few preliminary shots, was sufficient to convince Bougainville that his small force had best seek a safe haven, and he retreated rapidly.

In the city all was confusion, for Montcalm had been gravely wounded in the rout, and that night the wreckage of the French army streamed away up the river in flight. With the death of the gallant Montcalm—to complete as dramatic a battle as history records—and Townshend's energetic pressing of the siege, Quebec surrendered four days later ; and as its fall virtually gave Canada to Britain, so within a few years the removal of the French danger to the American colonies paved the way for their revolt, and thus to the creation of that vast new " seat of power " which Wolfe's vision had foreseen. He is known as the conqueror of Canada and as one of the progenitors of the British Empire ; he might equally be termed the grandfather of the United States. But if he had lived they might never have come into being, for with our knowledge of the way their struggle for independence hovered in the balance, for long tilting towards the British side, and of the half-heartedness of many in the revolting colonies, it is probable rather than possible that his decisive military action would have quelled the rebellion. We may go further : if his military operation had cut out the hostile growth, it is possible that a repetition of the wise and generous measures which he had recommended for French Canada might have healed the wound.

As a soldier, Wolfe's brief career makes it impossible to estimate his place among the Great Captains. Potentially he was among the greatest, and as a man had proved among the finest. Moreover, he had achieved the most masterly example in history of an amphibious operation, that combined " land and water " coup which is inherent in our traditions and the key to our world power ; which by exploiting the mobility given by our command of the sea for a sudden " bolt from the blue " endows our military striking forces with an influence out of all proportion to their slender size. And he had done enough to perpetuate the lesson that it is military genius and not mere competence

which decides the fate of nations.   To-day our
army is in its average of ability as high as in
Wolfe's day it was low, yet, and for this very
reason, it would be inherently impossible for
military genius to force its way to the front
at an early age ; and history tells us that genius
commonly flowers young.   Is the inference that
only a bad or an improvised army can produce
a great general.   Not only Wolfe, but Napoleon,
Moore, Wellington, Lee, and Stonewall Jackson
support it in modern times.   Another paradox
from the mystery of history.

Other titles of interest

ALEXANDER
Theodore Ayrault Dodge
723 pp., 234 illus., maps,
and charts
80690-8 $19.95

THE RISE OF U.S. GRANT
Colonel Arthur L. Conger
New introd. by Brooks D. Simpson
432 pp., 12 photos and 14 maps
80693-2 $15.95

THE GENERALSHIP OF
ULYSSES S. GRANT
J.F.C. Fuller
446 pp., 17 maps & plans
80450-6 $14.95

SHERMAN
Soldier, Realist, American
B. H. Liddell Hart
New foreword by Jay Luvaas
480 pp., 11 maps
80507-3 $15.95

THE ART OF WAR
Niccolò Machiavelli
Translated by Ellis Farneworth
Revised and with an introduction
by Neal Wood
336 pp.   80412-3 $12.95

FIFTEEN DECISIVE
BATTLES OF THE WORLD
From Marathon to Waterloo
Sir Edward S. Creasy
420 pp., 2 illus.   80559-6 $15.95

THE GENERALSHIP OF
ALEXANDER THE GREAT
J.F.C. Fuller
336 pp., 35 illus.,   80371-2 $14.95

HANNIBAL
Theodore Ayrault Dodge
702 pp., 227 charts, maps, plans,
and illus.   80654-1 $19.95

HANNIBAL
Enemy of Rome
Leonard Cottrell
287 pp., 27 illus., 10 maps
80498-0 $13.95

INVINCIBLE GENERALS
Philip J. Haythornthwaite
240 pp., 160 illus.,
29 maps and plans
80577-4 $16.95

LAWRENCE OF ARABIA
B. H. Liddell Hart
458 pp., 17 photos, 10 maps
80354-2 $13.95

THE ROMMEL PAPERS
Edited by B. H. Liddell Hart
544 pp., 17 photos
80157-4 $15.95

SCIPIO AFRICANUS
Greater than Napoleon
B. H. Liddell Hart
New foreword by Michael Grant
304 pp., 3 illus., 7 maps
80583-9 $13.95

MASTERS OF THE ART
OF COMMAND
Martin Blumenson and
James L. Stokebury
410 pp., 11 maps
80403-4 $14.95

Available at your bookstore

OR ORDER DIRECTLY FROM

DA CAPO PRESS, INC.

1-800-321-0050